365 DAILY DEVOTIONS

FOR A

DEDICATED TEACHER

INTRODUCTION

This book contains devotional readings for Christians who teach. The text is divided into 365 chapters, one for each day of the year. During the next year, try this experiment: read a chapter each day. If you're already committed to a daily time of worship, these readings will enrich that experience. If you are not, the simple act of giving God a few minutes each morning will change the tone and direction of your life.

Whether you teach graduate school or Sunday School, whether you lecture at seminary or at Vacation Bible School, you need and deserve a regularly scheduled conference with the ultimate Teacher. After all, you are God's emissary, a person charged with molding lives—a truly awesome responsibility. God takes your teaching duties very seriously, and so should you.

So if you are fortunate enough to find yourself in the role of teacher, accept a hearty congratulations and a profound word of thanks. And then, take a few moments to consider the promises and prayers on these pages. Remember that God honors your profession just as surely as He offers His loving abundance to you and your students. With God's help, you are destined to reshape eternity. It's a big job, but don't worry; you and God can handle it.

BECAUSE YOU'RE A TEACHER

Don't be in any rush to become a teacher, my friends. Teaching is highly responsible work. Teachers are held to the strictest standards.

James 3:1 MSG

As a teacher, you work hard, and your hard work pays off in the lives of your students. Daniel Webster wrote, "If we work in marble, it will perish; if we work upon brass, time will efface it; if we rear temples, they will crumble into dust; but if we work upon immortal minds and instill in them just principles, we are then engraving upon tablets which no time will efface, but which will brighten and brighten to all eternity." These words remind us of the glorious opportunities that are available to those who teach.

May you, with God's help, touch the hearts and minds of your students and, by doing so, refashion this wonderful world . . . and the next. And as you teach, may you always be a shining example to your students of the changes that Christ can make in the lives of those who love Him.

If you want a surefire way to reshape the future, here it is: find something important to say to the next generation . . . and say it.

Marie T. Freeman

HIS PROMISES

You will be a good servant of Christ Jesus, constantly nourished on the words of the faith and of the sound doctrine which you have been following.

1 Timothy 4:6 NASB

God has given us the Bible for the purpose of knowing His promises, His power, His commandments, His wisdom, His love, and His Son. As we study God's teachings and apply them to our lives, we live by the Word that shall never pass away.

Today, let us follow God's commandments, and let us conduct our lives in such a way that we might be shining examples to our students, to our families, and, most importantly, to those who have not yet found Christ.

The Bible was not given to increase our knowledge but to change our lives.

D. L. Moody

—TODAY'S PRAYER—

Heavenly Father, Your Word is a light unto the world; I will study it and trust it, and share it. In all that I do, help me be a worthy witness for You as I share the Good News of Your perfect Son and Your perfect Word. Amen

ABUNDANCE

My purpose is to give life in all its fullness.

John 10:10 Holman CSB

In the 10th chapter of John, when Jesus talks of the abundant life, is He talking about material riches or earthly fame? Hardly. The Son of God came to this world, not to give it prosperity, but to give it salvation. Thankfully for Christians, our Savior's abundance is both spiritual and eternal; it never falters—even if we do—and it never dies. We need only to open our hearts to Him, and His grace becomes ours.

God's gifts are available to all, but those gifts are not guaranteed; God's gifts must be claimed by those who choose to follow Christ. As we go about our daily lives, inside the classroom and out, may we accept God's promise of spiritual abundance, and may we share it with a world in desperate need of the Master's healing touch.

The only way you can experience abundant life is to surrender your plans to Him.

Charles Stanley

—TODAY'S PRAYER—

Dear Lord, You have offered me the gift of abundance through Your Son. Thank You, Father, for the abundant life that is mine through Christ Jesus. Let me accept His gifts and use them always to glorify You. Amen

GIFTS

This is why I remind you to keep using the gift God gave you when I laid my hands on you. Now let it grow, as a small flame grows into a fire.

2 Timothy 1:6 NCV

Perhaps you are one of those lucky teachers who has a natural gift for leading a class. But, even if you have the oratorical abilities of Winston Churchill and the intellectual capacities of Albert Einstein, you can still improve your teaching skills…and you should.

God's gifts are no guarantee of success; they must be cultivated and nurtured; otherwise they diminish over time. Today, accept this challenge: value the gift that God has given you, nourish it, make it grow, and share it with your students and with the world. After all, the best way to say "Thank You" for God's gifts is to use them.

One thing taught large in the Holy Scriptures is that while God gives His gifts freely, He will require a strict accounting of them at the end of the road. Each man is personally responsible for his store, be it large or small, and will be required to explain his use of it before the judgment seat of Christ.

A. W. Tozer

CHOICES

I have set before you life and death, blessing and curse. Choose life so that you and your descendants may live, love the Lord your God, obey Him, and remain faithful to Him. For He is your life, and He will prolong your life in the land the Lord swore to give to your fathers Abraham, Isaac, and Jacob.

Deuteronomy 30:19-20 Holman CSB

Life is a series of choices. From the instant we wake in the morning until the moment we nod off to sleep at night, we make countless decisions: decisions about the things we do, decisions about the words we speak, and decisions about the thoughts we choose to think. Simply put, the quality of those decisions determines the quality of our lives.

As you consider the next step in your life's journey—whether inside the classroom or outside it—take time to consider how many things in this life you can control: your thoughts, your words, your priorities, and your actions, for starters. And then, if you sincerely want to discover God's purpose for your life, make choices that are pleasing to Him. He deserves no less . . . and neither do you.

Freedom is not the right to do what we want but the power to do what we ought.

Corrie ten Boom

DISCOURAGEMENT

But as for you, be strong; don't be discouraged, for your work has a reward.

2 Chronicles 15:7 Holman CSB

When we fail to meet the expectations of others (or, for that matter, the expectations that we have set for ourselves), we may be tempted to abandon hope. Thankfully, on those cloudy days when our strength is sapped and our faith is shaken, there exists a source from which we can draw courage and wisdom. That source is God.

When we seek to form a more intimate and dynamic relationship with our Creator, He renews our spirits and restores our souls. God's promise is made clear in Isaiah 40:31: "But those who wait on the Lord shall renew their strength; They shall mount up with wings like eagles, They shall run and not be weary, They shall walk and not faint" (NKJV). And upon this promise we can—and should—depend.

Feelings of uselessness and hopelessness are not from God, but from the evil one, the devil, who wants to discourage you and thwart your effectiveness for the Lord.

Bill Bright

SOMETHING DONE FOR HIM

Whatever you do, do it enthusiastically, as something done for the Lord and not for men.

Colossians 3:23 Holman CSB

Sometimes, when the stresses of everyday life seem overwhelming, you may not feel very enthusiastic about yourself or your students.

If you're a teacher with too many obligations and too few hours in which to meet them, you are not alone. Teaching can be a demanding profession. But don't fret. Instead, focus upon God and upon His love for you. Then, ask Him for the strength you need to fulfill your responsibilities. God will give you the enthusiasm to do the most important things on today's to-do list if you ask Him. So ask Him. Now.

—TODAY'S PRAYER—

Lord, when the classroom leaves me exhausted, let me turn to You for strength and for renewal. When I follow Your will for my life, You will renew my enthusiasm. Let Your will be my will, Lord, and let me find my strength in You. Amen

IF YOU HAVE FAITH

If you do not stand firm in your faith, then you will not stand at all.

Isaiah 7:9 Holman CSB

Have you ever felt your faith in God slipping away? If so, you are not alone. Every life—including yours—is a series of successes and failures, celebrations and disappointments, joys and sorrows. But even when we feel very distant from God, God is never distant from us.

Jesus taught His disciples that if they had faith, they could move mountains. You can too. When you place your faith, your trust, indeed your life in the hands of Christ Jesus, you'll be amazed at the marvelous things He can do with you and through you. So strengthen your faith through praise, through worship, through Bible study, and through prayer. And trust God's plans. With Him, all things are possible, and He stands ready to open a world of possibilities to you if you have faith.

—TODAY'S PRAYER—

Lord, sometimes this world is a terrifying place. When I am filled with uncertainty and doubt, give me faith. In life's dark moments, help me remember that You are always near and that You can overcome any challenge. Today, Lord, and forever, I will place my trust in You. Amen

MOMENTS OF JOY

Always be full of joy in the Lord. I say it again—rejoice!
Philippians 4:4 NLT

As you plan for the upcoming day, are you making plans to celebrate? Hopefully so. After all, teaching can and should be a joyful experience. But as every veteran teacher knows, some days are more challenging than others. Nevertheless, even on the most difficult days, we can find pockets of satisfaction, islands of peace, and moments of joy.

Oswald Chambers correctly observed, "Joy is the great note all throughout the Bible." C. S. Lewis echoed that thought when he wrote, "Joy is the serious business of heaven."

Today, resolve to be a joyful Christian with a smile on your face and a song in your heart. After all, this is God's day, and He has given us clear instructions for its use. We are commanded to rejoice and be glad. So, with no further ado, let the celebration begin.

Joy is not the same as happiness—although they may overlap. Happiness depends on circumstances; joy depends on God.

Billy Graham

FORGIVING YOURSELF

The one who acquires good sense loves himself; one who safeguards understanding finds success.

Proverbs 19:8 Holman CSB

Are you perfect? Of course not! Even if you're an excellent teacher, you're bound to make mistakes and lots of them. When you make mistakes, here are a few things to remember 1. Be quick to apologize to the people you've hurt; 2. Be ready to fix the things you've broken; 3. Try to learn from your mistakes (the first time); 4. Ask God for His forgiveness (which, by the way, He will give to you instantly); 5. Forgive yourself; and 6. Don't dwell on the past; instead, get on with your life and your work. Class dismissed.

If you are in Christ, when he sees you, your sins are covered—he doesn't see them. He sees you better than you see yourself. And that is a glorious fact of your life.

Max Lucado

—TODAY'S PRAYER—

Dear Lord, sometimes I make mistakes and fall short of Your commandments. You have forgiven me, Father; let me forgive myself. When I disobey You, give me a repentant heart. And, whatever my circumstances, keep me mindful that I am Yours today, tomorrow, and forever. Amen

GOD'S CREATION

The heavens declare the glory of God, and the sky proclaims the work of His hands.

Psalm 19:1 Holman CSB

When we consider God's glorious universe, we marvel at the miracle of nature. The smallest seedlings and grandest stars are all part of God's infinite creation. God has placed His handiwork on display for all to see, and if we are wise, we will make time each day to celebrate the world that surrounds us.

Today, as you fulfill the demands of everyday life, pause to consider the majesty of heaven and earth. It is as miraculous as it is beautiful, as incomprehensible as it is breathtaking.

The Psalmist reminds us that the heavens are a declaration of God's glory. May we never cease to praise the Father for a universe that stands as an awesome testimony to His presence and His power.

—TODAY'S PRAYER—

Lord, when I stray from Your commandments, You offer me Your discipline and Your love. When I am wrong, You correct me in Your own way and in Your own time. I praise You for Your discipline, Father. Let me grow in the wisdom of Your ways, and let me live in accordance with Your will. Amen

GOD'S PROTECTION

If God is for us, who is against us?

Romans 8:31 Holman CSB

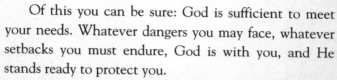

Of this you can be sure: God is sufficient to meet your needs. Whatever dangers you may face, whatever setbacks you must endure, God is with you, and He stands ready to protect you.

The Psalmist writes, "Weeping may endure for a night, but joy comes in the morning" (Psalm 30:5 NKJV). But when we are suffering, the morning may seem very far away. It is not. God promises that He is "near to those who have a broken heart" (Psalm 34:18 NKJV).

If you are experiencing the intense pain of a recent loss, or if you are still mourning a loss from long ago, perhaps the time has come to trust God and to reclaim the wonderful life He has given you.

There is not only fear, but terrible danger, for the life unguarded by God.

Oswald Chambers

—TODAY'S PRAYER—

Lord, You are my Shepherd. You care for me; You comfort me; You watch over me; and You have saved me. I will praise You, Father, for Your glorious works, for Your protection, for Your love, and for Your Son. Amen

HIS GRACE

But by the grace of God I am what I am, and his grace to me was not without effect. No, I worked harder than all of them—yet not I, but the grace of God that was with me.

1 Corinthians 15:10 NIV

Christ sacrificed His life on the cross so that we might have life eternal. This gift, freely given from God's only begotten Son, is the priceless possession of everyone who accepts Him as Lord and Savior. Thankfully, grace is not an earthly reward for righteous behavior; it is, instead, a blessed spiritual gift. When we accept Christ into our hearts, we are saved by His grace.

The familiar words from the book of Ephesians make God's promise perfectly clear: "It is by grace you have been saved . . . not by works, so that no one can boast" (2:8-9 NIV). God's grace is the ultimate gift, and we owe Him the ultimate in thanksgiving. Let us praise the Creator for His priceless gift, and let us share the Good News with friends, family members, students, and the world.

We return our Father's love by accepting His grace and by sharing His message and His love. When we do, we are eternally blessed. God is waiting patiently for each of us to accept the gift of eternal life. Let us claim His gift today.

IN ACCORDANCE WITH HIS PLAN

Those who listen to instruction will prosper; those who trust the LORD will be happy.

Proverbs 16:20 NLT

If you seek to live in accordance with God's plan for your life, you will study His Word, you will be attentive to His instructions, and you will be watchful for His signs. You will associate with fellow believers who, by their words and actions, will encourage your own spiritual growth. You will assiduously avoid those two terrible temptations: the temptation to sin and the temptation to squander time. And finally, you will listen carefully, even reverently, to the conscience that God has placed in your heart.

God has glorious plans for your day and your life. So as you go about your daily activities, keep your eyes and ears open . . . as well as your heart.

—TODAY'S PRAYER—

Dear Lord, let me choose Your plans. You created me, and You have called me to do Your work here on earth. Today, I choose to seek Your will and to live it, knowing that when I trust in You, I am eternally blessed. Amen

DOING HIS WILL

And this world is fading away, along with everything it craves. But if you do the will of God, you will live forever.

1 John 2:17 NLT

As human beings with limited understanding, we can never fully comprehend the will of God. But as believers in a benevolent God, we must always trust the will of our Heavenly Father.

Before His crucifixion, Jesus went to the Mount of Olives and poured out His heart to God (Luke 22). Jesus knew of the agony that He was destined to endure, but He also knew that God's will must be done. We, like our Savior, face trials that bring fear and trembling to the very depths of our souls, but like Christ, we, too, must ultimately seek God's will, not our own.

As this day unfolds, seek God's will for your own life and obey His Word. When you entrust your life to Him completely and without reservation, He will give you the strength to meet any challenge, the courage to face any trial, and the wisdom to live in His righteousness and in His peace.

—TODAY'S PRAYER—

Heavenly Father, in these quiet moments before this busy day unfolds, I come to You. I will study Your Word and seek Your guidance. Give me the wisdom to know Your will for my life and the courage to follow wherever You may lead me, today and forever. Amen

HAPPINESS

Obey God and be at peace with him; this is the way to happiness.

Job 22:21 NCV

Do you want to be happy? Here are some things you should do: Love God and His Son, Jesus; obey the Golden Rule; and always try to do the right thing. When you do these things, you'll discover that happiness goes hand-in-hand with good behavior.

The happiest people do not misbehave; the happiest people are not cruel or greedy. The happiest people don't say unkind things. The happiest people are those who love God and follow His rules—starting, of course, with the Golden one.

The happiest people in the world are not those who have no problems, but the people who have learned to live with those things that are less than perfect.

James Dobson

—TODAY'S PRAYER—

Lord, make me a happy Christian. Let me rejoice in the gift of this day, and let me praise You for the gift of Your Son. Make me be a joyful teacher, Lord, as I share Your Good News with all those who need Your healing touch. Amen

WE OVERESTIMATE

Humble yourselves therefore under the mighty hand of God, so that He may exalt you in due time, casting all your care upon Him, because He cares about you.

1 Peter 5:6-7 Holman CSB

Humility is not, in most cases, a naturally occurring human trait. Most of us, it seems, are more than willing to overestimate our own accomplishments. We are tempted to say, "Look how wonderful I am!" . . . hoping all the while that the world will agree with our own self-appraisals.

God honors humility . . . and He rewards those who humbly serve Him. When we acquired the wisdom to be humble, we bring enlightenment to the world (and blessings to ourselves).

But if we cannot overcome the tendency to overestimate our own accomplishments, then God still has some important lessons to teach us—lessons about the wisdom, the power, and the beauty of humility.

We can never have more of true faith than we have of true humility.

Andrew Murray

SHOUT THE NEWS

Now then we are ambassadors for Christ....

2 Corinthians 5:20 KJV

Are you a bashful Christian, one who is afraid to speak up for your Savior. Do you leave it up to others to share their testimonies while you stand on the sidelines, reluctant to share yours? Too many of us are slow to obey the last commandment of the risen Christ; we don't do our best to "make disciples of all the nations."

Christ's Great Commission applies to Christians of every generation, including our own. As believers, we are commanded to share the Good News with our families, with our neighbors, and with the world. Jesus invited His disciples to become fishers of men. We, too, must accept the Savior's invitation, and we must do so today. Tomorrow may indeed be too late.

—TODAY'S PRAYER—

Lord, even if I never leave home, make me a missionary for You. Let me share the Good News of Your Son, and let me tell of Your love and of Your grace. Make me a faithful servant for You, Father, now and forever. Amen

WORSHIP HIM ONLY

Trust in the Lord with all your heart, and do not rely on your own understanding; think about Him in all your ways, and He will guide you on the right paths.

Proverbs 3:5-6 Holman CSB

What does God require of us? That we worship Him only, that we welcome His Son into our hearts, and that we walk humbly with our Creator.

When Jesus was tempted by Satan, the Master's response was unambiguous. Jesus chose to worship the Lord and serve Him only. We, as followers of Christ, must follow in His footsteps.

When we place God in a position of secondary importance, we do ourselves great harm and we put ourselves at great risk. But when we place God squarely in the center of our lives—when we walk humbly and obediently with Him—we are blessed and we are protected.

Approach the Scriptures not so much as a manual of Christian principles but as the testimony of God's friends on what it means to walk with him through a thousand different episodes.

John Eldredge

POSSESSIONS

Then Jesus said to them, "Be careful and guard against all kinds of greed. Life is not measured by how much one owns."

Luke 12:15 NCV

Your material possessions are completely, utterly, and indisputably temporary. Every possession that you own will pass away, and soon. Thankfully, your spiritual possessions are not so fragile.

When you welcomed Christ into your heart, God promised that you would receive the gift of eternal life. The implications of that gift are beyond human understanding, but what you can understand is this: material wealth is inconsequential when compared to God's spiritual gifts.

Our ultimate aim in life is not to be healthy, wealthy, prosperous, or problem free. Our ultimate aim in life is to bring glory to God.

Anne Graham Lotz

—TODAY'S PRAYER—

Dear Lord, Your Word teaches me to seek first Your kingdom and Your righteousness. Today, I will trust You completely for my needs, both spiritual and material. Thank You, Father, for Your protection, for Your Love, and for Your Son. Amen

QUIET TIME

Be still, and know that I am God.

Psalm 46:10 NKJV

Face it: We live in a noisy world, a world filled with distractions, frustrations, and complications. But if we allow distractions—whether inside the classroom or outside it—to separate us from God's peace, we do ourselves a profound disservice.

Are you one of those busy teachers who rush through the day with scarcely a single moment for quiet contemplation and prayer? If so, it's time to reorder your priorities.

Nothing is more important than the time you spend with your Savior. So be still and claim the inner peace that is your spiritual birthright: the peace of Jesus Christ. It is offered freely; it has been paid for in full; it is yours for the asking. So ask. And then share.

As we find that it is not easy to persevere in this being "alone with God," we begin to realize that it is because we are not "wholly for God." God has a right to demand that He should have us completely for Himself.

Andrew Murray

HE DID IT FOR YOU

How shall we escape if we ignore such a great salvation? This salvation, which was first announced by the Lord, was confirmed to us by those who heard him.

Hebrews 2:3 NIV

How marvelous it is that God became a man and walked among us. Had He not chosen to do so, we might feel removed from a distant Creator. But ours is not a distant God. Ours is a God who understands—far better than we ever could—the essence of what it means to be human.

God understands our hopes, our fears, and our temptations. He understands what it means to be angry and what it costs to forgive. He knows the heart, the conscience, and the soul of every person who has ever lived, including you. And God has a plan of salvation that is intended for you. Accept it. Accept God's gift through the person of His Son Christ Jesus, and then rest assured: God walked among us so that you might have eternal life; amazing though it may seem, He did it for you.

Christ is the horn of our salvation, the One who was secured on a cross so that we could be secured in the Lamb's book of Life.

Beth Moore

YOUR ONGOING RELATIONSHIP

For You, O God, have tested us; You have refined us as silver is refined. You brought us into the net; You laid affliction on our backs. You have caused men to ride over our heads; we went through fire and through water; but You brought us out to rich fulfillment.

Psalm 66:10–12 NKJV

Your relationship with God is ongoing; it unfolds day by day, and it offers countless opportunities to grow closer to Him . . . or not. As each new day unfolds, you are confronted with a wide range of decisions: how you will behave, where you will direct your thoughts, with whom you will associate, and what you will choose to worship. These choices, along with many others like them, are yours and yours alone. How you choose determines how your relationship with God will unfold.

Are you continuing to grow in your love and knowledge of the Lord, or are you "satisfied" with the current state of your spiritual health? Hopefully, you're determined to make yourself a growing Christian. Your Savior deserves no less, and neither, by the way, do you.

As we spend time reading, applying, and obeying our Bibles, the Spirit of Truth Who is also the Spirit of Jesus increasingly reveals Jesus to us.

Anne Graham Lotz

TEMPTATION

Put on the full armor of God so that you can stand against the tactics of the Devil.

Ephesians 6:11 Holman CSB

How hard is it to bump into temptation in this crazy world? Not very hard. The devil, it seems, is causing pain and heartache in more places and in more ways than ever before. We, as Christians, must remain vigilant. Not only must we resist Satan when he confronts us, but we must also avoid those places where Satan can most easily tempt us. And, if we are to avoid the unending temptations of this world, we must earnestly wrap ourselves in the protection of God's Holy Word.

The road to ruin is wide, long, and deadly. Avoid it, and encourage your students do the same. When you do, God will smile—and the devil won't.

—TODAY'S PRAYER—

Dear Lord, this world is filled with temptations, distractions, and frustrations. When I turn my thoughts away from You and Your Word, Lord, I suffer bitter consequences. But, when I trust in Your commandments, I am safe. Direct my path far from the temptations and distractions of the world. Let me discover Your will and follow it, Dear Lord, this day and always. Amen

BEING UNDERSTOOD

The one who understands a matter finds success, and the one who trusts in the Lord will be happy.

Proverbs 16:20 Holman CSB

What a blessing it is when our loved ones genuinely seek to understand who we are and what we think. Just as we seek to be understood by others, so, too, should we seek to understand the hopes and dreams of our family members and students.

We live in a busy world, a place where it is all too easy to overlook the needs of others, but God's Word instructs us to do otherwise. In the Gospel of Matthew, Jesus declares, "In everything, therefore, treat people the same way you want them to treat you, for this is the Law and the Prophets" (Matthew 7:12 NASB).

Today, as you consider all the things that Christ has done in your life, honor Him by being a little kinder than necessary. Honor Christ by slowing down long enough to notice the trials and tribulations of your students. Honor Christ by giving the gift of understanding to friends and family. As a believer who has been eternally blessed by a loving Savior, you should do no less.

A religion that is small enough for our understanding would not be big enough for our needs.

Corrie ten Boom

YOUR DONATION

*Let this mind be in you which was also in Christ Jesus, who
. . . made Himself of no reputation, taking the form of a
bondservant, and coming in the likeness of men.*

Philippians 2:5,7 NKJV

If you genuinely want to make choices that are
pleasing to God, you must ask yourself this question:
"How does God want me to serve others?"

Whatever your age, wherever you happen to be, you
may be certain of this: service to others is an integral
part of God's plan for your life.

Every single day of your life, including this one,
God will give you opportunities to serve Him by serving
other people. Welcome those opportunities with open
arms. They are God's gift to you, His way of allowing you
to achieve greatness in His kingdom.

Determine to abide in Jesus wherever you are
placed.

Oswald Chambers

—TODAY'S PRAYER—

Heavenly Father, let my life be a life of service. You
have given me so many opportunities to serve. Let me
recognize those opportunities and seize them, today and
every day of my life. Amen

KNOWLEDGE

The fear of the Lord is the beginning of knowledge, but fools despise wisdom and discipline.

Proverbs 1:7 NIV

If we are to grow as Christians and as teachers, we need both knowledge and wisdom. Knowledge is found in textbooks. Wisdom, on the other hand, is found in God's Holy Word and in the carefully-chosen words of loving parents, family members, and friends.

Wisdom is not accumulated overnight. It is like a savings account that accrues slowly over time, and the person who consistently adds to his account will eventually accumulate a great sum. The secret to success is consistency.

Do you seek wisdom for yourself and for your students? Then keep learning and keep motivating them to do likewise. The ultimate source of wisdom, of course, is—first and foremost—the Word of God. When you begin a daily study of God's Word and live according to His commandments, you will become wise . . . and so, in time, will your students.

To know the will of God is the greatest knowledge! To do the will of God is the greatest achievement.

George W. Truett

GOD'S TIMING

Wait patiently on the Lord. Be brave and courageous. Yes, wait patiently on the Lord.

Psalm 27:14 NLT

Are you anxious for God to work out His plan for your life? Who isn't? As believers, we all want God to do great things for us and through us, and we want Him to do those things now. But sometimes, God has other plans. Sometimes, God's timetable does not coincide with our own. It's worth noting, however, that God's timetable is always perfect.

The next time you find your patience tested to the limit, remember that the world unfolds according to God's plan, not ours. Sometimes, we must wait patiently, and that's as it should be. After all, think about how patient God has been with us.

—TODAY'S PRAYER—

Dear Lord, Your wisdom is infinite, and the timing of Your Heavenly plan is perfect. You have a plan for my life that is grander than I can imagine. When I am impatient, remind me that You are never early or late. You are always on time, Father, so let me trust in You. Amen

THE ABUNDANT LIFE

And God is able to make every grace overflow to you, so that in every way, always having everything you need, you may excel in every good work.

2 Corinthians 9:8 Holman CSB

The 10th chapter of John reminds us of the abundance that can be ours through Christ. But what, exactly, did Jesus mean when He promised "life…more abundantly"? Was He referring to material possessions or financial wealth? Hardly. Jesus offers a different kind of abundance: a spiritual richness that extends beyond the temporal boundaries of this world. This everlasting abundance is available to all who seek it and claim it. May we, as believers, claim the riches of Christ Jesus every day that we live, and may we share His blessings with our students, with our families, with our coworkers, and with the world.

—TODAY'S PRAYER—

Heavenly Father, thank You for the abundant life that is mine through Christ Jesus. Guide me according to Your will, and help me to be a worthy servant in all that I say and do. Give me courage, Lord, to claim the rewards You have promised, and when I do, let the glory be Yours. Amen

ASK IN HIS NAME

Until now you have asked for nothing in My name. Ask and you will receive, that your joy may be complete.

John 16:24 Holman CSB

How often do you ask for God's help? Occasionally? Intermittently? Whenever you experience a crisis? Hopefully not. Hopefully, you have developed the habit of asking for God's assistance early and often. And hopefully, you have learned to seek His guidance in every aspect of your life.

God has promised that when you ask for His help, He will not withhold it. So ask. Ask Him to meet the needs of your day. Ask Him for wisdom. Ask Him to lead you, to protect you, and to correct you. And trust the answers He gives.

God stands at the door and waits. When you knock on His door, He answers. Your task, of course, is to seek His guidance prayerfully, confidently, and often.

Often I have made a request of God with earnest pleadings even backed up with Scripture, only to have Him say "No" because He had something better in store.

Ruth Bell Graham

USING TIME

The plans of the diligent certainly lead to profit, but anyone who is reckless only becomes poor.

Proverbs 21:5 Holman CSB

Time is a nonrenewable gift from God. How will you use it? You know from experience that you should invest some time each day in yourself, but finding time to do so is easier said than done. As a busy teacher, you may have difficulty investing large blocks of time in much-needed thought and self-reflection. If so, it may be time to reorder your priorities.

God has big plans for you. Discovering those plans will require trial and error, meditation and prayer, faith and perseverance. The moments of silence that you claim for yourself will help you gather your thoughts and sense direction from your Creator. And, the time that you spend discussing your dreams with friends and mentors can be invaluable.

Each waking moment holds the potential to think a creative thought or offer a heartfelt prayer. So even if you're a teacher with too many demands and too few hours in which to meet them, don't panic. Instead, be comforted in the knowledge that when you sincerely seek to discover God's purpose for your life, He will respond in marvelous and surprising ways. Remember: this is the day that He has made and that He has filled it with countless opportunities to love, to serve, and to seek His guidance.

WISE CHOICES

But seek first the kingdom of God and His righteousness, and all these things will be provided for you.

Matthew 6:33 Holman CSB

Because we are creatures of free will, we make choices—lots of them. When we make choices that are pleasing to our Heavenly Father, we are blessed. When we make choices that cause us to walk in the footsteps of God's Son, we enjoy the abundance that Christ has promised to those who follow Him. But when we make choices that are displeasing to God, we sow seeds that have the potential to bring forth a bitter harvest.

Today, as you encounter the challenges of everyday living, you will make hundreds of choices. Choose wisely. Make your thoughts and your actions pleasing to God. And remember: every choice that is displeasing to Him is the wrong choice—no exceptions.

Good and evil both increase at compound interest. That is why the little decisions you and I make every day are of such infinite importance.

C. S. Lewis

—TODAY'S PRAYER—

Dear Lord, help me make choices that are pleasing to You. Help me be honest, patient, and kind. And above all, help me follow the teachings of Jesus, not just today, but every day. Amen

CONFIDENCE

You are my hope; O Lord GOD, You are my confidence.
Psalm 71:5 NASB

We Christians have many reasons to be confident. God is in His heaven; Christ has risen, and we are the sheep of His flock. Yet sometimes, even the most devout Christians can become discouraged. Discouragement, however, is not God's way; He is a God of possibility not negativity.

Are you a confident Christian? You should be. God's grace is eternal and His promises are unambiguous. So count your blessings, not your hardships. And live courageously. God is the Giver of all things good, and He watches over you today and forever.

If we indulge in any confidence that is not grounded on the Rock of Ages, our confidence is worse than a dream, it will fall on us and cover us with its ruins, causing sorrow and confusion.

C. H. Spurgeon

—TODAY'S PRAYER—

Lord, when I place my confidence in the things of this earth, I will be disappointed. But, when I put my confidence in You, I am secure. In every aspect of my life, Father, let me place my hope and my trust in Your infinite wisdom and Your boundless grace. Amen

DECISIONS

Now if any of you lacks wisdom, he should ask God, who gives to all generously and without criticizing, and it will be given to him.

James 1:5 Holman CSB

Life presents each of us with countless questions, conundrums, doubts, and problems. Thankfully, the riddles of everyday living are not too difficult to solve if we look for answers in the right places. When we have questions, we should consult God's Word, we should seek the guidance of the Holy Spirit, and we should trust the counsel of God-fearing friends and family members.

Are you facing a difficult decision? Take your concerns to God and avail yourself of the messages and mentors that He has placed along your path. When you do, God will speak to you in His own way and in His own time, and when He does, you can most certainly trust the answers that He gives.

Every day, I find countless opportunities to decide whether I will obey God and demonstrate my love for Him or try to please myself or the world system. God is waiting for my choices.

Bill Bright

OVERCOMING DISCOURAGEMENT

The Lord is the One who will go before you. He will be with you; He will not leave you or forsake you. Do not be afraid or discouraged.

Deuteronomy 31:8 Holman CSB

Even the most devout Christians can become discouraged, and you are no exception. After all, you live in a world where expectations can be high and demands can be even higher.

If you find yourself enduring difficult circumstances, don't lose hope. If you face uncertainties about the future, don't become anxious. And if you become discouraged with the direction of your day or your life, don't despair. Instead, lift your thoughts and prayers to your Heavenly Father. He is a God of possibility, not negativity. You can be sure that He will guide you through your difficulties and beyond them . . . far beyond.

—TODAY'S PRAYER—

Heavenly Father, when I am discouraged, I will turn to You, and I will also turn to my Christian friends. I thank You, Father, for friends and family members who are willing to encourage me. I will acknowledge their encouragement, and I will share it. Amen

ENVY

For where envy and selfish ambition exist, there is disorder and every kind of evil.

James 3:16 Holman CSB

Because we are imperfect, we are sometimes envious of others. But to be envious is to be foolish. So we must guard ourselves against the natural tendency to feel resentment and jealousy when other people experience good fortune. Rather than succumbing to feelings of envy, we should focus on the marvelous things that God has done for us (and we should refrain from preoccupying ourselves with the blessings that God has chosen to give others).

St. John Chrysostom offered these words of caution: "As a moth gnaws a garment, so does envy consume a man." So here's a proven formula for a happier, healthier life: Count your own blessings and let your neighbors counts theirs. It's the best way to live.

—TODAY'S PRAYER—

Dear Lord, deliver me from the needless pain of envy. You have given me countless blessings. Let me be thankful for the gifts I have received, and let me never be resentful of the gifts You have given others. Amen

FAITH AND WHOLENESS

But he must ask in faith without any doubting, for the one who doubts is like the surf of the sea, driven and tossed by the wind.

James 1:6 NASB

As a dedicated member of the teaching profession—and as a thoughtful Christian—you should be amazed at the marvelous things Jesus can do.

When a suffering woman sought healing by simply touching the hem of His garment, Jesus turned and said, "Daughter, be of good comfort; thy faith hath made thee whole" (Matthew 9:22 KJV). We, too, can be made whole when we place our faith completely and unwaveringly in the person of Jesus Christ.

The Christian life is one of faith, where we find ourselves routinely overdriving our headlights but knowing it's okay because God is in control and has a purpose behind it.

Bill Hybels

—TODAY'S PRAYER—

Dear Lord, in the darkness of uncertainty, give me faith. In those moments when I am afraid, give me faith. When I am discouraged or confused, strengthen my faith in You. You are the Good Shepherd, let me trust in the perfection of Your plan and in the salvation of Your Son, this day and every day of my life. Amen

FINANCES

And my God shall supply all your need according to His riches in glory by Christ Jesus.

Philippians 4:19 NKJV

Countless books have been written about money—how to make it and how to keep it. But if you're a Christian, you probably already own at least one copy—and probably several copies—of the world's foremost guide to financial security. That book is the Holy Bible. God's Word is not only a roadmap to eternal life, it is also an indispensable guidebook for life here on earth. As such, the Bible has much to say about your life, your faith, and your finances.

If you're in need of a financial makeover, God's Word can help. In fact, Biblical principles can help you organize your financial life in such a way that you have less need to worry and more time to celebrate God's glorious creation. If that sounds appealing, open your Bible, read its instructions, and follow them.

I sincerely believe that once Christians have been educated in God's plan for their finances, they will find a freedom they had never known before.

Larry Burkett

FRIENDSHIP

How good and pleasant it is when brothers can live together!
Psalm 133:1 Holman CSB

What is a friend? The dictionary defines the word "friend" as "a person who is attached to another by feelings of affection or personal regard." This definition is accurate, as far as it goes, but when we examine the deeper meaning of friendship, so many more descriptors come to mind: trustworthiness, loyalty, helpfulness, kindness, understanding, forgiveness, encouragement, humor, and cheerfulness, to mention but a few.

How wonderful are the joys of friendship. Today, as you consider the many blessings that God has given you, remember to thank Him for the friends He has chosen to place along your path. May you be a blessing to them, and may they richly bless you today, tomorrow, and every day that you live.

—TODAY'S PRAYER—

Lord, You seek abundance and joy for me and for all Your children. One way that I can share Your joy is through the gift of friendship. Help me to be a loyal friend. Let me be ready to listen, ready to encourage, and ready to offer a helping hand. Keep me mindful that I am a servant of Your Son Jesus. Let me be a worthy servant, Lord, and a worthy friend. And, may the love of Jesus shine through me today and forever. Amen

SHAPING YOUR DAY

Yet, O LORD, you are our Father. We are the clay, you are the potter; we are all the work of your hand.

Isaiah 64:8 NIV

How do you begin your day? You most certainly should acquire the habit of giving God a few minutes of your time at the start of each day.

This morning and every morning hereafter, start your day with a time of prayer and consultation with the Giver of all things good. Prioritize your day according to God's commandments; seek His will first, and trust His wisdom. Then, you can face the day with the assurance that the same God who created our universe out of nothingness can help you place first things first in your own life.

An infinite God can give all of Himself to each of His children. He does not distribute Himself that each may have a part, but to each one He gives all of Himself as fully as if there were no others.

A. W. Tozer

When all else is gone, God is left, and nothing changes Him.

Hannah Whitall Smith

GOD'S FAITHFULNESS

God is faithful; by Him you were called into fellowship with His Son, Jesus Christ our Lord.

1 Corinthians 1:9 Holman CSB

God is faithful to us even when we are not faithful to Him. God keeps His promises to us even when we stray far from His path. God offers us countless blessings, but He does not force His blessings upon us. If we are to experience His love and His grace, we must claim them for ourselves.

God is with you. Listen prayerfully to the quiet voice of your Heavenly Father. Talk with God often; seek His guidance; watch for His signs; listen to the wisdom that He shares through the reliable voice of your own conscience.

God loves you, and you deserve all the best that God has to offer. You can claim His blessings today by being faithful to Him.

Are you serious about wanting God's guidance to become a personal reality in your life? The first step is to tell God that you know you can't manage your own life; that you need his help.

Catherine Marshall

HE LEADS

The LORD says, "I will guide you along the best pathway for your life. I will advise you and watch over you."

Psalm 32:8 NLT

Psalm 37 teaches us that, "The steps of the Godly are directed by God. He delights in every detail of their lives" (v. 22 NLT). In other words, God is intensely interested in each of us, and He will guide our steps if we serve Him obediently.

When we sincerely offer heartfelt prayers to our Heavenly Father, He will give direction and meaning to our lives—but He won't force us to follow Him. To the contrary, God has given us the free will to follow His commandments . . . or not.

When we stray from God's commandments, we invite bitter consequences. But, when we follow His commandments, and when we genuinely and humbly seek His will, He touches our hearts and leads us on the path of His choosing.

Will you trust God to guide your steps? You should. When you entrust your life to Him completely and without reservation, God will give you the strength to meet any challenge, the courage to face any trial, and the wisdom to live in His righteousness and in His peace. So trust Him today and seek His guidance. When you do, your next step will be the right one.

GRATITUDE NOW

As you therefore have received Christ Jesus the Lord, so walk in Him, having been firmly rooted and now being built up in Him and established in your faith, just as you were instructed, and overflowing with gratitude.

Colossians 2:6-7 NASB

The words of 1 Thessalonians 5:18 remind us to give thanks in every circumstance of life. But sometimes, when our hearts are troubled and our lives seem to be spinning out of control, we don't feel much like celebrating. Yet God's Word is clear: In all circumstances, our Father offers us His love, His strength, and His Grace. And, in all circumstances, we must thank Him.

Have you thanked God today for blessings that are too numerous to count? Have you offered Him your heartfelt prayers and your wholehearted praise? If not, it's time to slow down and offer a prayer of thanksgiving to the One who has given you life on earth and life eternal.

If you are a thoughtful Christian, you will be a thankful Christian. No matter your circumstances, you owe God so much more than you can ever repay, and you owe Him your heartfelt thanks. So thank Him . . . and keep thanking Him, today, tomorrow and forever.

HONEST WITH OURSELVES

The honest person will live in safety . . . .

Proverbs 10:9 NCV

The old saying is both familiar and true: Honesty is, indeed, the best policy. But, honesty is not just the best policy, it is also God's policy. and if we are to obey commandments that God has given us, we must be honest with others and with ourselves. Truth is not just the best way, it is also His way.

God doesn't expect you to be perfect, but he does insist on complete honesty.

Rick Warren

We can teach our children that being honest protects from guilt and provides for a clear conscience.

Josh McDowell

—TODAY'S PRAYER—

Dear Lord, You command Your children to walk in truth. Let me be honest with others and with myself. Honesty isn't just the best policy, Lord; it's Your policy, and I will obey You by making it my policy, too. Amen

LOVE IS A CHOICE

If I speak the languages of men and of angels, but do not have love, I am a sounding gong or a clanging cymbal.

1 Corinthians 13:1 Holman CSB

Love is always a choice. Sometimes, of course, we may "fall in love," but it takes work to stay there. Sometimes, we may be "swept off our feet," but the "sweeping" is only temporary; sooner or later, if love is to endure, one must plant one's feet firmly on the ground. The decision to love another person for a lifetime is much more than the simple process of "falling in" or "being swept up." It requires "reaching out," "holding firm," and "lifting up." Love, then, becomes a decision to honor and care for the other person, come what may.

Inasmuch as love grows in you, so beauty grows. For love is the beauty of the soul.

St. Augustine

Love always means sacrifice.

Elisabeth Elliot

—TODAY'S PRAYER—

Lord, love is Your commandment. Help me always to remember that the gift of love is a precious gift indeed. Let me nurture love and treasure it. And, keep me mindful that the essence of love is not to receive it, but to give it, today and forever. Amen

TREASURE

For what will it profit a man if he gains the whole world, and loses his own soul? Or what will a man give in exchange for his soul?

Mark 8:36-37 NKJV

All of mankind is engaged in a colossal, worldwide treasure hunt. Some people seek treasure from earthly sources, treasures such as material wealth or public acclaim; others seek God's treasures by making Him the cornerstone of their lives.

What kind of treasure hunter are you? Are you so caught up in the demands of everyday living that you sometimes allow the search for worldly treasures to become your primary focus? If so, it's time to think long and hard about what you value, and why.

All the items on your daily to-do list are not created equal. That's why you must do the hard work of putting first things first. And the "first things" in life definitely have less to do with material riches and more to do with riches of the spiritual kind.

The more we stuff ourselves with material pleasures, the less we seem to appreciate life.

Barbara Johnson

OPPORTUNITY

Therefore, as we have opportunity, we must work for the good of all, especially for those who belong to the household of faith.

Galatians 6:10 Holman CSB

As each day unfolds, we are literally surrounded by more opportunities than we can count—opportunities to improve our own lives and the lives of those we love. Each of us possess the ability to experience earthly peace and spiritual abundance, but sometimes peace and abundance seem to be little more than distant promises.

As we face the challenges that are part of life here on earth, we must not become discouraged. We must instead arm ourselves with the promises of God. When we do, we can expect the very best that life—and God—has to offer.

Do you expect the coming day to be a fountain of opportunities? Are you expecting the best (and preparing yourself for it), or are you expecting the worst (and bracing yourself against it)? The answer to these questions will have a profound and surprising influence on the quality of your day and your life.

God specializes in things fresh and firsthand. His plans for you this year may outshine those of the past. He's prepared to fill your days with reasons to give Him praise.

Joni Eareckson Tada

PERFECTIONISM

Those who wait for perfect weather will never plant seeds; those who look at every cloud will never harvest crops. Plant early in the morning, and work until evening, because you don't know if this or that will succeed. They might both do well.

Ecclesiastes 11:4,6 NCV

As you begin to work toward improved physical and emotional health, don't expect perfection. Of course you should work hard; of course you should be disciplined; of course you should do your best. But then, when you've given it your best effort, you should be accepting of yourself, imperfect though you may be.

In heaven, we will know perfection. Here on earth, we have a few short years to wrestle with the challenges of imperfection. Let us accept these lives that God has given us—and these bodies which are ours for a brief time here on earth—with open, loving arms.

—TODAY'S PRAYER—

Lord, this world has so many expectations of me, but today I will not seek to meet the world's expectations; I will do my best to meet Your expectations. I will make You my ultimate priority, Lord, by serving You, by praising You, by loving You, and by obeying You. Amen

YOUR BEST

The thing you should want most is God's kingdom and doing what God wants. Then all these other things you need will be given to you.

Matthew 6:33 NCV

God deserves your best. Is He getting it? Do you make an appointment with your Heavenly Father each day? Do carve out moments when He receives your undivided attention? Or is your devotion to Him fleeting, distracted, and sporadic?

When you acquire the habit of focusing your heart and mind squarely upon God's intentions for your life, He will guide your steps and bless your endeavors. But if you allow distractions to take priority over your relationship with God, they will—and you will pay a price for your mistaken priorities.

Today, focus upon God's Word and upon His will for your life. When you do, you'll be amazed at how quickly everything else comes into focus, too.

How important it is for us—young and old—to live as if Jesus would return any day—to set our goals, make our choices, raise our children, and conduct business with the perspective of the imminent return of our Lord.

Gloria Gaither

RIGHTEOUSNESS

As for you, if you walk before Me as your father David walked, with integrity of heart and uprightness, doing everything I have commanded you, and if you keep My statutes and ordinances, I will establish your royal throne over Israel forever, as I promised your father David.

1 Kings 9:4-5 Holman CSB

Oswald Chambers, the author of the Christian classic, *My Utmost For His Highest*, advised, "Never support an experience which does not have God as its source, and faith in God as its result." These words serve as a powerful reminder that, as Christians, we are called to walk with God and to obey His commandments. But, we live in a world that presents countless temptations for adults and even more temptations for our students.

As leaders in the classroom, we must teach our students that the choices they make are never without consequence. When they choose wisely, they reap bountiful rewards. But, when they behave foolishly, they invite pain and disappointment into their lives.

As Christian teachers, we must instruct our students by word and by example. And our instructions from God are clear: when confronted with sin, we must walk—or better yet run—in the opposite direction. When we do, we reap the blessings that God has promised to all those who live according to His will and His Word.

HE IS OUR STRENGTH

The Lord is my strength and my song; He has become my salvation.

Exodus 15:2 Holman CSB

Where do you turn for strength? Do you depend upon the world's promises or, for that matter, upon your own resources? Or do you turn toward God for the wisdom and strength to meet to challenges of the coming day? The answer should be obvious: God comes first.

Each morning, before you become caught up in the complexities of everyday life, spend meaningful moments with your Creator. Offer Him your prayers and study His Word. When you offer God the firstfruits of your day, you gain wisdom, perspective, and strength.

The same God who empowered Samson, Gideon, and Paul seeks to empower my life and your life, because God hasn't changed.

Bill Hybels

—TODAY'S PRAYER—

Dear Lord, whenever I feel discouraged or tired, I will turn to You for strength. I know that when I open my heart to You, Father, You will renew my strength and my enthusiasm. Let Your will be my will, Lord, and let me find my strength in You. Amen

ANXIETY

Cast all your anxiety on him because he cares for you.

1 Peter 5:7 NIV

God calls us to live above and beyond anxiety. God calls us to live by faith, not by fear. He instructs us to trust Him completely, this day and forever. But sometimes, trusting God is difficult, especially when we become caught up in the incessant demands of an anxious world.

When you feel anxious—and you will—return your thoughts to God's love. Then, take your concerns to Him in prayer, and to the best of your ability, leave them there. Whatever "it" is, God is big enough to handle it. Let Him. Now.

Anxiety may be natural and normal for the world, but it is not to be part of a believer's lifestyle.

Kay Arthur

—TODAY'S PRAYER—

Father, sometimes troubles and distractions preoccupy thoughts and trouble my soul. When I am anxious, Lord, let me turn my prayers to You. When I am worried, give me faith in You. Let me live courageously, Dear God, knowing that You love me and that You will protect me, today and forever. Amen

POWERFUL PRESCRIPTIONS

For I am not ashamed of the gospel, because it is God's power for salvation to everyone who believes.

Romans 1:16 Holman CSB

As a spiritual being, you have the potential to grow in your personal knowledge of the Lord every day that you live. You can do so through prayer, through worship, through an openness to God's Holy Spirit, and through a careful study of God's Holy Word.

Your Bible contains powerful prescriptions for everyday living. If you sincerely seek to walk with God, you should commit yourself to the thoughtful study of His teachings. The Bible can and should be your roadmap for every aspect of your life.

Do you seek to establish a closer relationship with your Heavenly Father? Then study His Word every day, with no exceptions. The Holy Bible is a priceless, one-of-a-kind gift from God. Treat it that way and read it that way.

The balance of affirmation and discipline, freedom and restraint, encouragement and warning is different for each child and season and generation, yet the absolutes of God's Word are necessary and trustworthy no matter how mercuric the time.

Gloria Gaither

CHARACTER IS . . .

May integrity and uprightness protect me, because my hope is in you.

Psalm 25:21 NIV

Character is built slowly over a lifetime. It is the sum of every right decision, every honest word, every noble thought, and every heartfelt prayer. It is forged on the anvil of honorable work and polished by the twin virtues of generosity and humility. Character is a precious thing—difficult to build but easy to tear down. As believers in Christ, we must seek to live each day with discipline, honesty, and faith. When we do, integrity becomes a habit. And God smiles.

Character means living your life before God, fearing only Him, and seeking to please Him alone, no matter how you feel or what others may say or do.

Warren Wiersbe

—TODAY'S PRAYER—

Dear Lord, make me a teacher whose conduct is honorable. Make me a teacher whose words are true. Give me the wisdom to know right from wrong, and give me the courage—and the skill—to do what needs to be done in the service of Your Son. Amen

SHARING WORDS OF HOPE

Blessed be the God and Father of our Lord Jesus Christ, the Father of mercies and the God of all comfort. He comforts us in all our affliction, so that we may be able to comfort those who are in any kind of affliction, through the comfort we ourselves receive from God.

2 Corinthians 1:3-4 Holman CSB

We live in a world that is, at times, a frightening place. We live in a world that is, at times, a discouraging place. We live in a world where life-changing losses can be so painful and so profound that it seems we will never recover. But, with God's help, and with the help of encouraging family members and friends, we can recover.

When it is our family, friends, or students who must endure hardships, our obligation is clear. As men and women who have been comforted by the promises of Christ, we must share words of encouragement, assurance, perspective, and hope.

Discouraged people don't need critics. They hurt enough already. They don't need more guilt or piled-on distress. They need encouragement. They need a refuge, a willing, caring, available someone.

Charles Swindoll

COUNTING YOUR BLESSINGS

Obey My voice, and I will be your God, and you shall be my people. And walk in all the ways that I have commanded you, that it may be well with you.

Jeremiah 7:23 NKJV

If you sat down and began counting your blessings, how long would it take? A very, very long time! Your blessings include life, freedom, family, friends, talents, possessions, and, of course, the opportunity that you have been given to become a teacher. But, your greatest blessing—a gift that is yours for the asking—is God's gift of salvation through Christ Jesus. Today, give thanks for your blessings and share them. When you do, God will smile . . . and so will your students.

Blessings can either humble us and draw us closer to God or allow us to become full of pride and self-sufficiency.

Jim Cymbala

—TODAY'S PRAYER—

Dear Lord, let me count my blessings and help my students count theirs. You have richly blessed my life, Lord. Let me, in turn, be a blessing to all those who cross my path, and may the glory be Yours forever. Amen

MID-COURSE CORRECTIONS

For now we see indistinctly, as in a mirror, but then face to face. Now I know in part, but then I will know fully, as I am fully known.

1 Corinthians 13:12 Holman CSB

No lesson plan is perfect; sometimes, savvy teachers must make mid-course corrections during class . . . or else! And so it is with life: Sometimes, we must make major modifications in our hopes, dreams, goals, and plans . . . or else.

Some of our most important dreams are the ones we abandon. Some of our most important goals are the ones we don't attain. Sometimes, our most important journeys are the ones that we take to the winding conclusion of what seems to be dead end streets. Thankfully, with God there are no dead ends; there are only opportunities to learn, to yield, to trust, to serve, and to grow.

The next time you experience one of life's inevitable disappointments, don't despair and don't be afraid to try "Plan B." Consider every setback an opportunity to choose a different, more appropriate path. Have faith that God may indeed be leading you in an entirely different direction, a direction of His choosing. And as you take your next step, remember that what looks like a dead end to you may, in fact, be the fast lane according to God.

HOPEFUL HEARTS

I want their hearts to be encouraged and joined together in love, so that they may have all the riches of assured understanding, and have the knowledge of God's mystery—Christ.

Colossians 2:2 Holman CSB

Each day provides countless opportunities to encourage others and to praise their good works. When we do, we not only spread seeds of joy and happiness, we also follow the commandments of God's Holy Word. The 118th Psalm reminds us, "This is the day which the Lord hath made; we will rejoice and be glad in it" (v. 24 KJV). As we rejoice in this day that the Lord has given us, let us remember that an important part of today's celebration is the time we spend celebrating others.

How can we build others up? By celebrating their victories and their accomplishments. So look for the good in others and celebrate the good that you find. When you do, you'll be a powerful force of encouragement in the world…and a worthy servant to your God.

A lot of people have gone further than they thought they could because someone else thought they could.

Zig Ziglar

EXCUSES

Now the one who plants and the one who waters are equal, and each will receive his own reward according to his own labor.

1 Corinthians 3:8 Holman CSB

Your work is a picture book of your priorities. So whatever your teaching assignment, it's up to you, and no one else, to become masterful at your profession. It's up to you to do your job right, and to do it right now. It's time for excellence, not excuses.

Because we humans are such creative excuse-makers, all of the best excuses have already been taken—we've heard them all before.

So if you're ever tempted to concoct a new and improved excuse, don't bother. It's impossible. A far better strategy is this: do the work. Now. Then, let your excellent work speak loudly and convincingly for itself.

Replace your excuses with fresh determination.

Charles Swindoll

—TODAY'S PRAYER—

Heavenly Father, how easy it is to make excuses. But, I want to be a teacher who accomplishes important work for You. Help me, Father, to strive for excellence, not excuses. Amen

FEAR

Do not fear, for I am with you; do not be afraid, for I am your God. I will strengthen you; I will help you; I will hold on to you with My righteous right hand.

Isaiah 41:10 Holman CSB

We live in a fear-based world, a world where bad news travels at light speed and good news doesn't. These are troubled times, times when we have legitimate fears for the future of our nation, our world, and our families. But as Christians, we have every reason to live courageously. After all, the ultimate battle has already been fought and won on that faraway cross at Calvary.

Perhaps you, like countless other believers, have found your courage tested by the anxieties and fears that are an inevitable part of 21st-Century life. If so, God wants to have a little chat with you. The next time you find your courage tested to the limit, God wants to remind you that He is not just near; He is here.

Your Heavenly Father is your Protector and your Deliverer. Call upon Him in your hour of need, and be comforted. Whatever your challenge, whatever your trouble, God can handle it. And will.

God alone can give us songs in the night.

C. H. Spurgeon

THE COMMANDMENT TO FORGIVE

And forgive us our sins, for we ourselves also forgive everyone in debt to us.

Luke 11:4 Holman CSB

Forgiveness is God's commandment, but oh how difficult a commandment it can be to follow. Being frail, fallible, imperfect human beings, we are quick to anger, quick to blame, slow to forgive, and even slower to forget. No matter. Forgiveness, although difficult, is God's way.

Teachers, having been placed in positions of leadership, serve as important role models to their students. As such, teachers must be models of forgiveness, both inside the classroom and out. We must, on occasion, forgive those who have injured us; to do otherwise is to disobey God.

—TODAY'S PRAYER—

Lord, I know that forgiveness is Your commandment, but genuine forgiveness is difficult indeed. I feel the strong desire to strike out at those who have hurt me, but You command me to refrain from bitterness and to turn away from revenge. Help me to forgive others, Lord, just as You have forgiven me. Keep me mindful, Lord, that I am never fully liberated until I have been freed from the prison of hatred, and that You offer freedom from that prison through Your Son, Jesus Christ. Amen

GENEROSITY

So let each one give as he purposes in his heart, not grudgingly or of necessity; for God loves a cheerful giver.

2 Corinthians 9:7 NKJV

Are you a cheerful giver? If you intend to obey God's commandments, you must be. When you give, God looks not only at the quality of your gift, but also at the condition of your heart. If you give generously, joyfully, and without complaint, you obey God's Word. But, if you make your gifts grudgingly, or if the motivation for your gift is selfish, you disobey your Creator, even if you have tithed in accordance with Biblical principles.

Today, take God's commandments to heart and make this pledge: Be a cheerful, generous, courageous giver. The world needs your help, and you need the spiritual rewards that will be yours when you give faithfully, prayerfully, and cheerfully.

It's not difficult to make an impact on your world. All you really have to do is put the needs of others ahead of your own. You can make a difference with a little time and a big heart.

James Dobson

HE DIRECTS

A man's heart plans his way, but the Lord directs his steps.

Proverbs 16:9 NKJV

God has a plan for your life. He understands that plan as thoroughly and completely as He knows you. And, if you seek God's will earnestly and prayerfully, He will make His plans known to you in His own time and in His own way.

If you sincerely seek to live in accordance with God's will for your life, you will live in accordance with His commandments. You will study God's Word, and you will be watchful for His signs.

Sometimes, God's plans seem unmistakably clear to you. But other times, He may lead you through the wilderness before He directs you to the Promised Land. So be patient and keep seeking His will for your life. When you do, you'll be amazed at the marvelous things that an all-powerful, all-knowing God can do.

—TODAY'S PRAYER—

Lord, today, I will seek Your will for my life. You have a plan for me, Father. Let me discover it and live it, knowing that when I trust in You, I am eternally blessed. Amen

THE SAME FOR THEM

Just as you want others to do for you, do the same for them.
Luke 6:31 Holman CSB

The words of Luke 6:31 remind us that, as believers in Christ, we are commanded to treat others as we wish to be treated. This commandment is, indeed, the Golden Rule for Christians of every generation. When we weave the thread of kindness into the very fabric of our lives, we give glory to the One who gave His life for us.

The Golden Rule starts at home, but it should never stop there.

Marie T. Freeman

If we have the true love of God in our hearts, we will show it in our lives. We will not have to go up and down the earth proclaiming it. We will show it in everything we say or do.

D. L. Moody

—TODAY'S PRAYER—

Dear Lord, the Golden Rule is not only a perfect standard to use with my friends and neighbors, it is also a guide for teaching my students. Enable me to respect my students as I want them to respect me. Help me to walk in their shoes and to see life from their perspective. Help me, Father, to be a nurturing, loving teacher every day that I live, and may the glory be yours. Amen

HEALTH

Therefore, brothers, by the mercies of God, I urge you to present your bodies as a living sacrifice, holy and pleasing to God; this is your spiritual worship.

Romans 12:1 Holman CSB

Are you concerned about your spiritual, physical, or emotional health? If so, there is a timeless source of comfort and assurance that is as near as your next breath. That source of comfort, of course, is God.

God is concerned about every aspect of your life, including your health. And, when you face concerns of any sort—including health-related challenges—God is with you. So trust your medical doctor to do his or her part, and turn to your family and friends for moral, physical, and spiritual support. But don't be afraid to place your ultimate trust in your benevolent Heavenly Father. His healing touch, like His love, endures forever.

A Christian should no more defile his body than a Jew would defile the temple.

Warren Wiersbe

—TODAY'S PRAYER—

Lord, when I am ill, or weak, or troubled, You heal me. Renew me, Father, and let me trust Your will for my life. Let me welcome Your unending love and Your healing touch, now and forever. Amen

THE JOYS OF TEACHING

I have spoken these things to you so that My joy may be in you and your joy may be complete.

John 15:11 Holman CSB

Teaching should be a joyful experience, but every teacher knows that some days are so busy and so hurried that abundance seems a distant promise. It is not. Every day, we can claim the spiritual abundance and joy that God promises for our lives…and we should.

C. H. Spurgeon, the renowned 19th century English clergymen, advised, "Rejoicing is clearly a spiritual command. To ignore it, I need to remind you, is disobedience." As Christians, we are called by our Creator to live abundantly, prayerfully, and joyfully. To do otherwise is to squander His spiritual gifts.

If, today, your heart is heavy, open the door of your soul to the Father and to His only begotten Son. Christ offers you His peace and His joy. Accept it and share it freely, just as Christ has freely shared His joy with you.

—TODAY'S PRAYER—

Dear Lord, You are my loving Heavenly Father, and You created me in Your image. As Your faithful child, I will make Your joy my joy. I will praise Your works, I will obey Your Word, and I will honor Your Son, this day and every day of my life. Amen

MISSIONS

But you will receive power when the Holy Spirit has come upon you, and you will be My witnesses in Jerusalem, in all Judea and Samaria, and to the ends of the earth.

Acts 1:8 Holman CSB

As Christians, we are all called to share the Good News of Jesus Christ. We are commanded to reach out to those in need and to share the Gospel with our communities and with the world. The need for evangelism is always urgent, and the workers are always few.

Are you doing your part to share Christ's message? It's a question only you can answer, and it's a question that you should answer today.

We are now, a very, very few feeble workers, scattering the grain broadcast according as time and strength permit. God will give the harvest; doubt it not. But the laborers are few.

Lottie Moon

—TODAY'S PRAYER—

Lord, make me a missionary for You in word and deed. Let me teach the Good News of Your Son, and let me tell of Your love and of Your grace. Make me a faithful servant for You, Father, now and forever. Amen

PATIENCE

Be gentle to everyone, able to teach, and patient.
2 Timothy 2:23 Holman CSB

The teaching profession requires heaping helpings of patience, understanding, forgiveness, and poise. Sometimes, students are impulsive; sometimes, they misbehave; oftentimes, students under-perform; sometimes, they simply don't show up at all.

Despite the inevitable shortcomings of their students, savvy teachers maintain their composure—even when students or parents don't.

Our world is filled with imperfect people; so are our classrooms. All of us, students and faculty members alike, make our share of mistakes. God commands us to respond to the shortcomings of others with patience, understanding, forgiveness, and love—which, by the way, is exactly how God has already responded to us.

If you want to hear God's voice clearly and you are uncertain, then remain in His presence until He changes that uncertainty. Often much can happen during this waiting for the Lord. Sometimes He changes pride into humility; doubt into faith and peace . . . .

Corrie ten Boom

PERSPECTIVE

But Martha was pulled away by all she had to do in the kitchen. Later, she stepped in, interrupting them. "Master, don't you care that my sister has abandoned the kitchen to me? Tell her to lend me a hand." The Master said, "Martha, dear Martha, you're fussing far too much and getting yourself worked up over nothing. One thing only is essential, and Mary has chosen it—it's the main course, and won't be taken from her."

Luke 10:40-42 MSG

Sometimes, amid the demands of daily life, we lose perspective. Life seems out of balance, and the pressures of everyday living seem overwhelming. What's needed is a fresh perspective, a restored sense of balance...and God. If we call upon the Lord and seek to see the world through His eyes, He will give us guidance and wisdom and perspective. When we make God's priorities our priorities, He will lead us according to His plan and according to His commandments. God's reality is the ultimate reality. May we live accordingly.

Joy is the direct result of having God's perspective on our daily lives and the effect of loving our Lord enough to obey His commands and trust His promises.

Bill Bright

REGRET

And don't be wishing you were someplace else or with someone else. Where you are right now is God's place for you. Live and obey and love and believe right there.

1 Corinthians 7:17 MSG

Bitterness can destroy you if you let it . . . so don't let it! If you are caught up in intense feelings of anger or regret, you know all too well the destructive power of these emotions. How can you rid yourself of these feelings? First, you must prayerfully ask God to free you from these feelings. Then, you must learn to catch yourself whenever thoughts of bitterness begin to attack you. Your challenge is this: You must learn to resist negative thoughts before they hijack your emotions.

Christina Rossetti had this sound advice: "Better by far you should forget and smile than you should remember and be sad." And she was right—it's better to forget than regret.

The enemy of our souls loves to taunt us with past failures, wrongs, disappointments, disasters, and calamities. And if we let him continue doing this, our life becomes a long and dark tunnel, with very little light at the end.

Charles Swindoll

WHEN HE RETURNS

But the Day of the Lord will come like a thief; on that day the heavens will pass away with a loud noise, the elements will burn and be dissolved, and the earth and the works on it will be disclosed . . . . Therefore, dear friends, while you wait for these things, make every effort to be found in peace without spot or blemish before Him.

2 Peter 3:10,14 Holman CSB

When will our Lord return? The Bible clearly states that the day and the hour of Christ's return is known only to God. Therefore, we must conduct our lives as if He were returning today.

If Jesus were to return this instant, would you be ready? Would you be proud of your actions, your thoughts, your relationships, and your prayers? If not, you must face up to a harsh reality: even if Christ does not return to earth today, He may call you home today! And if He does so, you must be prepared.

Have you given your heart to the resurrected Savior? If the answer to that question is anything other than an unqualified yes, then accept Him as your personal Savior before you close this book.

The fact that Jesus Christ is to come again is not a reason for star-gazing, but for working in the power of the Holy Ghost.

C. H. Spurgeon

SPIRITUAL GROWTH

Therefore, leaving the elementary message about the Messiah, let us go on to maturity.

Hebrews 6:1 Holman CSB

The journey toward spiritual maturity lasts a lifetime: As Christians, we can and should continue to grow in the love and the knowledge of our Savior as long as we live. Norman Vincent Peale had simple advice for believers of all ages: "Ask the God who made you to keep remaking you." That advice, of course, is perfectly sound, but too often ignored.

When we cease to grow, either emotionally or spiritually, we do ourselves and our families a profound disservice. But, if we study God's Word, if we obey His commandments, and if we live in the center of His will, we will not be "stagnant" believers; we will, instead, be growing Christians . . . and that's exactly what God wants for our lives.

In those quiet moments when we open our hearts to God, the Creator who made us keeps remaking us. He gives us direction, perspective, wisdom, and courage. And, the appropriate moment to accept His spiritual gifts is always this one.

As I have continued to grow in my Christian maturity, I have discovered that the Holy Spirit does not let me get by with anything.

Anne Graham Lotz

TESTIMONY

Be wise in the way you act with people who are not believers, making the most of every opportunity.

Colossians 4:5 NCV

In his second letter to Timothy, Paul offers a message to believers of every generation when he writes, "God has not given us a spirit of timidity" (1:7 NASB). Paul's meaning is crystal clear: When sharing our testimonies, we, as Christians, must be courageous, forthright, and unashamed.

We live in a world that desperately needs the healing message of Christ Jesus. Every believer, each in his or her own way, bears a personal responsibility for sharing that message. If you are a believer in Christ, you know how He has touched your heart and changed your life. Now it's your turn to share the Good News with others. And remember: today is the perfect time to share your testimony because tomorrow may quite simply be too late.

Although our actions have nothing to do with gaining our own salvation, they might be used by God to save somebody else! What we do really matters, and it can affect the eternities of people we care about.

Bill Hybels

UNITY

Above all, put on love—the perfect bond of unity.
Colossians 3:14 Holman CSB

When like-minded believers worship together and work together, great things happen. When godly men and women join together in unity, they can build bridges inside their churches and beyond.

Are you a builder of bridges inside your fellowship and throughout your community? If so, you can be sure that God will smile upon your endeavors. And you can be sure that He will bless you—and your fellowship—in surprising, miraculous ways.

It never ceases to amaze me the way the Lord creates a bond among believers which reaches across continents, beyond race and color.

Corrie ten Boom

The Lord Jesus Christ enables us all to be family.
Dennis Swanberg

—TODAY'S PRAYER—

Lord, so much more can be accomplished when we join together to fulfill our common goals and desires. As I seek to fulfill Your will for my life, let me also join with others to accomplish Your greater good for our nation and for all humanity. Amen

THE SHOUT OF FAITH

For in it God's righteousness is revealed from faith to faith,
just as it is written: The righteous will live by faith.

Romans 1:17 Holman CSB

Hannah Whitall Smith advised, "Shout the shout of faith. Nothing can withstand the triumphant faith that links itself to omnipotence. For 'this is the victory that overcometh the world.' The secret of all successful living lies in this shout of faith." Christian teachers agree.

So, if your faith is being tested, know that your Savior is near. If you reach out to Him in faith, He will give you peace, perspective, and hope. If you are content to touch even the smallest fragment of the Master's garment, He will make you whole.

Faith has no value of its own, it has value only as it connects us with Him. It is a trick of Satan to get us occupied with examining our faith instead of resting in the Faithful One.

Vance Havner

=—TODAY'S PRAYER—

Dear Lord, help me strengthen my faith—and share it—today and every day of my life. Amen

KINDNESS

And be kind and compassionate to one another, forgiving one another, just as God also forgave you in Christ.

Ephesians 4:32 Holman CSB

In the busyness and stress of a teacher's demanding day, it is easy to become frustrated. We are imperfect human beings struggling to manage our lives as best we can, but sometimes we fall short. When we are distracted or disappointed, we may neglect to share a kind word or a kind deed. This oversight hurts others, and it hurts us as well.

Christ's words are straightforward: "I tell you the truth, anything you did for even the least of my people here, you also did for me" (Matthew 25:40 NCV). For believers, then, the message is clear: When we share a word of encouragement with a student or extend the hand of friendship to a peer, God smiles.

—TODAY'S PRAYER—

Lord, make me a loving, encouraging Christian. And, let my love for Christ be reflected through the kindness that I show to my students, to my family, to my friends, and to all who need the healing touch of the Master's hand. Amen

GOD'S CALLING

I pray that the eyes of your heart may be enlightened so you may know what is the hope of His calling, what are the glorious riches of His inheritance among the saints, and what is the immeasurable greatness of His power to us who believe, according to the working of His vast strength.

Ephesians 1:18-19 Holman CSB

It is terribly important that you heed God's calling by discovering and developing your talents and your spiritual gifts. If you seek to make a difference—and if you seek to bear eternal fruit—you must discover your gifts and begin using them for the glory of God.

Every believer has at least one gift. In John 15:16, Jesus says, "You did not choose Me, but I chose you and appointed you that you should go and bear fruit, and that your fruit should remain, that whatever you ask the Father in My name He may give you." Have you found your special calling? If not, keep searching and keep praying until you find it. God has important work for you to do, and the time to begin that work is now.

If God has called you, do not spend time looking over your shoulder to see who is following you.

Corrie ten Boom

EVERYONE WHO BELIEVES

Everyone who believes that Jesus is the Messiah has been born of God...

1 John 5:1 Holman CSB

God loves you. Period. And His affection for you is deeper and more profound than you can imagine. God's love for you is so great that He sent His only Son to this earth to die for your sins and to offer you the priceless gift of eternal life. Now, you must decide whether or not to accept God's gift. Will you ignore it or embrace it? Will you return it or neglect it? Will you accept Christ or not? The decision, of course, is yours and yours alone, and the decision has eternal consequences. Accept God's gift: Accept Christ.

It's your heart that Jesus longs for: your will to be made His own with self on the cross forever, and Jesus alone on the throne.

Ruth Bell Graham

—TODAY'S PRAYER—

Father, You gave Your Son that I might have life eternal. Thank You for this priceless gift and for the joy I feel in my heart when I give You my thoughts, my prayers, my praise, and my life. Amen

HOW GODLY TEACHERS BEHAVE

Lead a tranquil and quiet life in all godliness and dignity.

1 Timothy 2:2 Holman CSB

Teachers serve as powerful examples to their students. Wise teachers understand that while words often fall upon closed ears, actions do not. And, godly teachers behave accordingly.

Are you determined to be a teacher whose words and deeds are worthy of your heavenly Father and His only begotten Son? The answer to that question will determine the quality and direction of your life both inside and outside the classroom.

Live in such a way that any day would make a suitable capstone for life. Live so that you need not change your mode of living, even if your sudden departure were immediately predicted to you.

C. H. Spurgeon

—TODAY'S PRAYER—

Lord, I pray that my actions will always be consistent with my beliefs. I know that my deeds speak more loudly than my words. May every step that I take reflect Your truth and love, and may others be drawn to You because of my words and my deeds. Amen

TAKE COURAGE

For God has not given us a spirit of fearfulness, but one of power, love, and sound judgment.

2 Timothy 1:7 Holman CSB

Courage builds character and vice versa. So if you'd like a brief course in character-building, try this: the next time you face a choice between doing the right thing or the easy thing, summon the courage to do the right thing. And while you're summoning that courage, ask God to help.

Billy Graham observed, "Down through the centuries, in times of trouble and trial, God has brought courage to the hearts of those who love Him. The Bible is filled with assurances of God's help and comfort in every kind of trouble which might cause fears to arise in the human heart. You can look ahead with promise, hope, and joy." Dr. Graham's words apply to you.

The next time you find your courage tested by the inevitable challenges of life, remember that God is as near as your next breath. He is your shield and your strength; He is your protector and your deliverer. Call upon Him in your hour of need and then be comforted. Whatever your challenge, whatever your trouble, God can handle it. And will.

Take courage. We walk in the wilderness today and in the Promised Land tomorrow.

D. L. Moody

THANKS BE TO GOD

Thanks be to God for His indescribable gift.

2 Corinthians 9:15 Holman CSB

God sent His Son to transform the world and to save it. The Christ Child was born in the most humble of circumstances: in a nondescript village, to parents of simple means, far from the seats of earthy power.

God sent His Son, not as a conqueror or a king, but as an innocent babe. Jesus came, not to be served, but to serve. Jesus did not preach a message of retribution or revenge; He spoke words of compassion and forgiveness. We must do our best to imitate Him.

In the second chapter of Luke, we read about shepherds who were tending their flocks on the night Christ was born. May we, like those shepherds of old, leave our fields—wherever they may be—and pause to worship God's priceless gift: His only begotten Son.

Today Jesus Christ is being dispatched as the Figurehead of a Religion, a mere example. He is that, but He is infinitely more; He is salvation itself, He is the Gospel of God.

Oswald Chambers

DRAW NEAR

Let us draw near with a true heart in full assurance of faith, our hearts sprinkled clean from an evil conscience and our bodies washed in pure water.

Hebrews 10:22 Holman CSB

American humorist Josh Billings observed, "Reason often makes mistakes, but conscience never does." How true. Even when we deceive our neighbors, and even when we attempt to deceive ourselves, God has given each of us a conscience, a small, quiet voice that tells us right from wrong. We must listen to that inner voice . . . or else we must accept the consequences that inevitably befall those who choose to rebel against God.

God desires that we become spiritually healthy enough through faith to have a conscience that rightly interprets the work of the Holy Spirit.

Beth Moore

—TODAY'S PRAYER—

Dear Lord, You speak to me through the Bible, through the words of others, and through that still, small voice within. Through my conscience, You reveal Your will and Your way for my life. In these quiet moments, show me Your plan for this day, Heavenly Father, that I might serve You. Amen

PREPARED?

He awakens Me morning by morning, He awakens My ear to hear as the learned. The Lord God has opened My ear.
Isaiah 50:4-5 NKJV

How do you prepare for the day ahead? Do you awaken early enough to spend at least a few moments with God? Or do you sleep until the last possible minute, leaving no time to invest in matters of the heart and soul? Hopefully, you make a habit of spending precious moments each morning with your Creator. When you do, He will fill your heart, He will direct your thoughts, and He will guide your steps.

Your daily devotional time can be habit-forming, and should be. The first few minutes of each day are invaluable. Treat them that way, and offer them to God.

Meditating upon His Word will inevitably bring peace of mind, strength of purpose, and power for living.

Bill Bright

—TODAY'S PRAYER—

Lord, help me to hear Your direction for my life in the quiet moments when I study Your Holy Word. And as I go about my daily activities, let everything that I say and do be pleasing to You. Amen

DOUBTS

Now if any of you lacks wisdom, he should ask God, who gives to all generously and without criticizing, and it will be given to him. But let him ask in faith without doubting. For the doubter is like the surging sea, driven and tossed by the wind.

James 1:5-6 Holman CSB

Doubts come in several shapes and sizes: doubts about God, doubts about the future, and doubts about our own abilities, for starters. But when doubts creep in, as they will from time to time, we need not despair. As Sheila Walsh observed, "To wrestle with God does not mean that we have lost faith, but that we are fighting for it."

God never leaves our side, not for an instant. He is always with us, always willing to calm the storms of life. When we sincerely seek His presence—and when we genuinely seek to establish a deeper, more meaningful relationship Him—God is prepared to touch our hearts, to calm our fears, to answer our doubts, and to restore our confidence.

Mark it down. God never turns away the honest seeker. Go to God with your questions. You may not find all the answers, but in finding God, you know the One who does.

Max Lucado

THE ETERNAL FUTURE

And this is the testimony: God has given us eternal life, and this life is in His Son. The one who has the Son has life. The one who doesn't have the Son of God does not have life.

1 John 5:11-12 Holman CSB

Your ability to envision the future, like your life here on earth, is limited. God's vision, however, is not burdened by any such limitations. He sees all things, He knows all things, and His plans for you endure for all time.

God's plans are not limited to the events of life-here-on-earth. Your Heavenly Father has bigger things in mind for you . . . much bigger things. So praise the Creator for the gift of eternal life and share the Good News with all who cross your path. You have given your heart to the Son, so you belong to the Father—today, tomorrow, and for all eternity.

God loves you and wants you to experience peace and life—abundant and eternal.

Billy Graham

Let us see the victorious Jesus, the conqueror of the tomb, the one who defied death. And let us be reminded that we, too, will be granted the same victory.

Max Lucado

WHEN YOU ARE TESTED

Jesus answered them, "I assure you: If you have faith and do not doubt, you will not only do what was done to the fig tree, but even if you tell this mountain, 'Be lifted up and thrown into the sea,' it will be done."

Matthew 21:21 Holman CSB

Concentration camp survivor Corrie ten Boom relied on faith during her long months of imprisonment and torture. Later, despite the fact that four of her family members had died in Nazi death camps, Corrie's faith was unshaken. She wrote, "There is no pit so deep that God's love is not deeper still." Christians take note: Genuine faith in God means faith in all circumstances, happy or sad, joyful or tragic.

If your faith is being tested to the point of breaking, remember that your Savior is near. If you reach out to Him in faith, He will give you peace and heal your broken spirit. Reach out today. If you touch even the smallest fragment of the Master's garment, He will make you whole.

To fear and not be afraid, that is the paradox of faith.

A. W. Tozer

FITNESS

Whatever you do, do everything for God's glory.
1 Corinthians 10:31 Holman CSB

Are you shaping up or spreading out? Do you eat sensibly and exercise regularly, or do you spend most of your time on the couch with a Twinkie in one hand and a clicker in the other? Are you choosing to treat your body like a temple or a trash heap? How you answer these questions will help determine how long you live and how well you live.

Physical fitness is a choice, a choice that requires discipline—it's as simple as that. So, do yourself this favor: treat your body like a one-of-a-kind gift from God . . . because that's precisely what your body is.

You can't buy good health at the doctor's office—you've got to earn it for yourself.

Marie T. Freeman

—TODAY'S PRAYER—

Lord, all that I am belongs to You. As I serve You with all that I am and all that I have, help me to honor You by caring for the body that You have given me. Amen

WHAT IS A FRIEND?

A friend loves you all the time, and a brother helps in time of trouble.

Proverbs 17:17 NCV

What is a friend? The dictionary defines the word friend as "a person who is attached to another by feelings of affection or personal regard." This definition is accurate, as far as it goes, but when we examine the deeper meaning of friendship, so many more descriptors come to mind: trustworthiness, loyalty, helpfulness, kindness, understanding, forgiveness, encouragement, humor, and cheerfulness, to mention but a few.

How wonderful are the joys of friendship. Today, as you consider the many blessings that God has given you, remember to thank Him for the friends He has chosen to place along your path. May you be a blessing to them, and may they richly bless you today, tomorrow, and every day that you live.

—TODAY'S PRAYER—

Thank You Lord, for the Friend I have in Jesus. And, thank You for the dear friends You have given me, the friends who enrich my life. I pray for them today, and ask Your blessings upon them. Amen

HE MADE ETERNITY

Only fools say in their hearts "There is no God."

Psalm 14:1 NLT

God is eternal and unchanging. Before He laid the foundations of our universe, He was a being of infinite power and love, and He will remain so throughout all eternity.

We humans are in a state of constant change. We are born, we grow, we mature, and we die. Along the way, we experience the inevitable joys and hardships of life. And we face the inevitable changes that are the result of our own mortality.

But God never changes. His love never ceases, His wisdom never fails, and His promises endure, unbroken, forever.

God did not spring forth from eternity; He brought forth eternity.

C. H. Spurgeon

The unfolding of our friendship with the Father will be a never-ending revelation stretching on into eternity.

Catherine Marshall

GOD'S LOVE

This is what real love is: It is not our love for God; it is God's love for us in sending his Son to be the way to take away our sins.

1 John 4:10 NCV

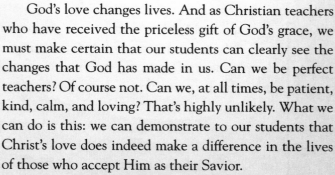

God's love changes lives. And as Christian teachers who have received the priceless gift of God's grace, we must make certain that our students can clearly see the changes that God has made in us. Can we be perfect teachers? Of course not. Can we, at all times, be patient, kind, calm, and loving? That's highly unlikely. What we can do is this: we can demonstrate to our students that Christ's love does indeed make a difference in the lives of those who accept Him as their Savior.

God's grace is the ultimate gift, and we owe Him the ultimate in thanksgiving. Let us praise the Creator for His priceless gift; let us share His Good News; and let us live according to His commandments. When we do, our students will be blessed with powerful, godly role models. And we will be transformed, not only for a day, but also for all eternity.

God is a God of unconditional, unremitting love, a love that corrects and chastens but never ceases.

Kay Arthur

THE CORNERSTONE?

You are the God who works wonders; You revealed Your strength among the peoples.

Psalm 77:14 Holman CSB

Have you made God the cornerstone of your life, or is He relegated to a few hours on Sunday morning? Have you genuinely allowed God to reign over every corner of your heart, or have you attempted to place Him in a spiritual compartment? The answer to these questions will determine the direction of your day and your life.

God loves you. In times of trouble, He will comfort you; in times of sorrow, He will dry your tears. When you are weak or sorrowful, God is as near as your next breath. He stands at the door of your heart and waits. Welcome Him in and allow Him to rule. And then, accept the peace, and the strength, and the protection, and the abundance that only God can give.

—TODAY'S PRAYER—

Lord, sometimes life is difficult. Sometimes, I am worried, weary, or discouraged. The classroom can be a struggle, but, when I lift my eyes to You, Father, You strengthen me. Today, I will turn to You, Lord, for strength, for hope, and for salvation. Amen

THE GREAT COMMISSION

But the eleven disciples proceeded to Galilee, to the mountain which Jesus had designated. When they saw Him, they worshiped Him; but some were doubtful. And Jesus came up and spoke to them, saying, "All authority has been given to Me in heaven and on earth. "Go therefore and make disciples of all the nations, baptizing them in the name of the Father and the Son and the Holy Spirit, teaching them to observe all that I commanded you; and lo, I am with you always, even to the end of the age."

Matthew 28:16–20 NASB

After His resurrection, Jesus addressed His disciples. As recorded in the 28th chapter of Matthew, Christ instructed His followers to share His message with the world. This "Great Commission" applies to Christians of every generation, including our own.

As believers, we are called to share the Good News of Jesus with our families, with our neighbors, and with the world. Christ commanded His disciples to become fishers of men. We must do likewise, and we must do so today. Tomorrow may indeed be too late.

Missions is God finding those whose hearts are right with Him and placing them where they can make a difference for His kingdom.

Henry Blackaby

THE WISDOM OF HOPE

Let us hold on to the confession of our hope without wavering, for He who promised is faithful.

Hebrews 10:23 Holman CSB

Along with other lessons, we must teach our students the wisdom of hope. There are few sadder sights than that of a thoroughly discouraged young person. As teachers, we cannot control the emotions of our students, but we can help our students learn to think optimistically about themselves and about their opportunities.

Hope, like plants in a garden, must be cultivated with care. If we leave our hopes untended—or if we contaminate them with the twin poisons of discouragement and doubt—the gardens of our souls produce few fruits. But, if we nurture our hopes through a firm faith in God and a realistic faith in ourselves, we bring forth bountiful harvests that bless us, our families, ours students, and generations yet unborn.

Without the certainty of His resurrection, we would come to the end of this life without hope, with nothing to anticipate except despair and doubt. But because He lives, we rejoice, knowing soon we will meet our Savior face to face, and the troubles and trials of this world will be behind us.

Bill Bright

LOVE

Dear friends, since God loved us that much, we surely ought to love each other.

1 John 4:11 NLT

Love, like everything else in this wonderful world, begins and ends with God, but the middle part belongs to us. During the brief time that we have here on earth, God has given each of us the opportunity to become a loving person—or not. God has given each of us the opportunity to be kind, to be courteous, to be cooperative, and to be forgiving—or not. God has given each of us the chance to obey the Golden Rule, or to make up our own rules as we go. If we obey God's rules, we're safe, but if we do otherwise, we're headed for trouble and fast.

Here in the real world, the choices that we make have consequences. The decisions that we make and the results of those decisions determine the quality of our relationships. It's as simple as that.

—TODAY'S PRAYER—

Lord, You have given me the gift of eternal love; let me share that gift with my students and with the world. Help me, Father, to show kindness to those who cross my path and make me generous with words of encouragement and praise. And, help me always to reflect the love that Christ Jesus gave me so that through me, others might find Him. Amen

MATURITY

When I was a child, I spoke like a child, I thought like a child, I reasoned like a child. When I became a man, I put aside childish things.

1 Corinthians 13:11 Holman CSB

If only our students would behave maturely and responsibly, teaching would be a breeze. But, here in the real world, young people don't grow into mature adults overnight. What's a teacher to do? Be patient, be understanding, and be demanding. Teachers who allow undisciplined behavior to go unchecked are doing a disservice to their students. God does not reward laziness nor does He praise mediocrity, and neither should we.

Be patient. God is using today's difficulties to strengthen you for tomorrow. He is equipping you. The God who makes things grow will help you bear fruit.

Max Lucado

—TODAY'S PRAYER—

Thank You, Lord, that I am not yet what I am to become. The Holy Scripture tells me that You are at work in my life, continuing to help me grow and to mature in the faith. Show me Your wisdom, Father, and let me share Your wisdom with my students and with the world. Amen

OPTIMISM

Lord, I turn my hope to You. My God, I trust in You.
Psalm 25:1-2 Holman CSB

Christians have every reason to be optimistic about life. As John Calvin observed, "There is not one blade of grass, there is no color in this world that is not intended to make us rejoice." But sometimes, when we are tired or frustrated, rejoicing seems only a distant promise. Thankfully, God stands ready to restore us: "I will give you a new heart and put a new spirit in you…" (Ezekiel 36:26 NIV). Our task, of course, is to let Him.

Today, accept the new spirit that God seeks to infuse into your heart. Think optimistically about yourself, your students, your school, and your world. Rejoice in this glorious day that the Lord has given you, and share your optimism with others. Your enthusiasm will be contagious, and your words will bring healing and comfort to a world that needs both.

The essence of optimism is that it takes no account of the present, but it is a source of inspiration, of vitality, and of hope. Where others have resigned, it enables a man to hold his head high, to claim the future for himself, and not abandon it to his enemy.

Dietrich Bonhoeffer

THE PEACE OF CHRIST

Let the peace of Christ rule in your hearts, since as members of one body you were called to peace.

Colossians 3:15 NIV

We frail human beings lose hope from time to time. When we do, we need the encouragement of friends and the life-changing power of prayer.

If we find ourselves falling into the spiritual traps of worry, discouragement, or despair, we should seek direction from God, and we should solicit the encouraging words of friends and family members. God has promised that peace, and joy are ours to claim . . . and we should take whatever steps are necessary to claim these gifts.

Juliana of Norwich noted that, "Peace and love are always alive in us, but we are not always alive to peace and love." Our task, simply put, is to guard ourselves from the spiritual traps that might entrap us . . . and then to claim the peace, the love, and the power that can—and should—be ours.

In the center of a hurricane there is absolute quiet and peace. There is no safer place than in the center of the will of God.

Corrie ten Boom

PROCRASTINATION

We can't afford to waste a minute, must not squander these precious daylight hours in frivolity and indulgence, in sleeping around and dissipation, in bickering and grabbing everything in sight. Get out of bed and get dressed! Don't loiter and linger, waiting until the very last minute. Dress yourselves in Christ, and be up and about!

Romans 13:13-14 MSG

Once the season for planting is upon us, the time to plant seeds is when we make time to plant seeds. And when it comes to planting God's seeds in the soil of eternity, the only certain time that we have is now. Yet because we are fallible human beings with limited vision and misplaced priorities, we may be tempted to delay.

If we hope to reap a bountiful harvest for God, for our families, and for ourselves, we must plant now by defeating a dreaded human frailty: the habit of procrastination. Procrastination often results from our shortsighted attempts to postpone temporary discomfort.

A far better strategy is this: Whatever "it" is, do it now. When you do, you won't have to worry about "it" later.

Never fail to do something because you don't feel like it. Sometimes you just have to do it now, and you'll feel like it later.

Marie T. Freeman

A GUIDE FOR LIFE

For the eyes of the Lord are on the righteous, and His ears are open to their prayers; but the face of the Lord is against those who do evil.

1 Peter 3:12 NKJV

Do you desire to be a righteous person? Are you bound and determined—despite the inevitable temptations and distractions of our modern age—to be an example of godly behavior to your family, to your friends, and to your students? If so, you must hunger and thirst for righteousness. You must yearn to be righteous; you must strive to be righteous; and you must work to be righteous by putting aside many of the things that the world holds dear.

You will never become righteous by accident. You must hunger for righteousness, and when you do, you will be filled.

Have your heart right with Christ, and he will visit you often, and so turn weekdays into Sundays, meals into sacraments, homes into temples, and earth into heaven.

C. H. Spurgeon

SILENCE

Be silent before the Lord and wait expectantly for Him.
Psalm 37:7 Holman CSB

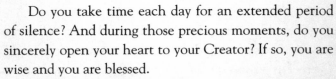

Do you take time each day for an extended period of silence? And during those precious moments, do you sincerely open your heart to your Creator? If so, you are wise and you are blessed.

The world can be a noisy place, a place filled to the brim with distractions, interruptions, and frustrations. And if you're not careful, the struggles and stresses of everyday living can rob you of the peace that should rightfully be yours because of your personal relationship with Christ. So take time each day to quietly commune with your Savior. When you do, those moments of silence will enable you to participate more fully in the only source of peace that endures: God's peace.

—TODAY'S PRAYER—

Dear Lord, in the quiet moments of this day, I will turn my thoughts and prayers to You. In silence, I will sense Your presence, and I will seek Your will for my life, knowing that when I accept Your peace, I will be blessed today and throughout eternity. Amen

YOUR GIFT TO GOD

Every good gift and every perfect gift is from above, and cometh down from the Father of lights.

James 1:17 KJV

The old saying is both familiar and true: "What we are is God's gift to us; what we become is our gift to God." Each of us possess special talents, gifted by God, that can be nurtured carefully or ignored totally. Our challenge, of course, is to use our abilities to the greatest extent possible and to use them in ways that honor our Savior.

Are you using your natural talents to make God's world a better place? If so, congratulations. But if you have gifts that you have not fully explored and developed, perhaps you need to have a chat with the One who gave you those gifts in the first place. Your talents are priceless treasures offered from your Heavenly Father. Use them. After all, an obvious way to say "thank you" to the Giver is to use the gifts He has given.

If you want to reach your potential, you need to add a strong work ethic to your talent.

John Maxwell

QUICK ANGER

Don't become angry quickly, because getting angry is foolish.

Ecclesiastes 7:9 NCV

The frustrations of everyday living can sometimes get the better of us, and we allow minor disappointments to cause us major problems. When we allow ourselves to become overly irritated by the inevitable ups and downs of life, we become overstressed, overheated, over-anxious, and just plain angry.

When you allow yourself to become angry, you are certain to defeat at least one person: yourself. When you allow the minor frustrations of everyday life to hijack your emotions, you do harm to yourself and to your loved ones. So today and every day, guard yourself against the kind of angry thinking that inevitably takes a toll on your emotions and your relationships.

As the old saying goes, "Anger usually improves nothing but the arch of a cat's back." So don't allow feelings of anger or frustration to rule your life, or, for that matter, your day—your life is simply to short for that, and you deserve much better treatment than that . . . from yourself.

Bitterness and anger, usually over trivial things, make havoc of homes, churches, and friendships.

Warren Wiersbe

HIS BOOK, YOUR OBEDIENCE

But grow in the grace and knowledge of our Lord and Savior Jesus Christ. To Him be the glory both now and forever. Amen.

2 Peter 3:18 NKJV

Too many Christians treat the Bible like any other book. But get this loud and clear: THE BIBLE ISN'T LIKE ANY OTHER BOOK! Period! And if you're wise, you'll give your Bible the reverence and the attention that it deserves.

Is God's Word a bright spotlight that guides your path, or is it a tiny night light that occasionally flickers? Is God's Word your indispensable compass for everyday living, or is it relegated to Sunday morning services? Do you read the Bible faithfully or sporadically? The answer to these questions will determine the direction of your thoughts, the direction of your day, and the direction of your life.

God's Word can be a roadmap to a place of righteousness and abundance. Make it your roadmap. God's wisdom can be a light to guide your steps. Claim it as your light today, tomorrow, and every day of your life—and then walk confidently in the footsteps of God's only begotten Son.

CHEERFUL?

Is anyone cheerful? He should sing praises.

James 5:13 Holman CSB

Few things in life are more sad, or, for that matter, more absurd, than a grumpy Christian. Christ promises us lives of abundance and joy, but He does not force His joy upon us. We must claim His joy for ourselves, and when we do, Jesus, in turn, fills our spirits with His power and His love.

How can we receive from Christ the joy that is rightfully ours? By giving Him what is rightfully His: our hearts and our souls.

When we earnestly commit ourselves to the Savior of mankind, and when we place Jesus at the center of our lives and trust Him as our personal Savior, He will transform us, not just for today, but for all eternity. Then we, as God's children, can share Christ's joy and His message with a world that needs both.

The people whom I have seen succeed best in life have always been cheerful and hopeful people who went about their business with a smile on their faces.

Charles Kingsley

COMFORTING OTHERS

Even when I go through the darkest valley, I fear [no] danger, for You are with me.

Psalm 23:4 Holman CSB

We live in a world that is, on occasion, a frightening place. Sometimes, we sustain life-altering losses that are so profound and so tragic that it seems we could never recover. But, with God's help and with the help of encouraging family members and friends, we can recover.

In times of need, God's Word is clear: as believers, we must offer comfort to those in need by sharing not only our courage but also our faith. As the renowned revivalist Vance Havner observed, "No journey is complete that does not lead through some dark valleys. We can properly comfort others only with the comfort wherewith we ourselves have been comforted of God."

In times of adversity, we are wise to remember the words of Jesus, who, when He walked on the waters, reassured His disciples, saying, "Take courage! It is I. Don't be afraid" (Matthew 14:27 NIV). Then, with Christ on His throne—and with trusted friends and loving family members at our sides—we can face our fears with courage and with faith.

HE GOES BEFORE

The Lord is the One who will go before you. He will be with you; He will not leave you or forsake you. Do not be afraid or discouraged.

Deuteronomy 31:8 Holman CSB

Life can be difficult and discouraging at times. During our darkest moments, we can depend upon our friends and family, and upon God. When we do, we find the courage to face even the darkest days with hopeful hearts and willing hands.

Are you ready to do as God asks and lay all your pain, desires, fears, and hopes on Him? If so, then you will discover a newfound strength, compliments of God.

So when you find yourself worried about the challenges of today or the uncertainties of tomorrow, you must ask yourself whether or not you are ready to place your concerns and your life in God's all-powerful, all-knowing, all-loving hands. If the answer to that question is yes—as it should be—then you can draw courage today from the source of strength that never fails: your Heavenly Father.

With each new experience of letting God be in control, we gain courage and reinforcement for daring to do it again and again.

Gloria Gaither

BEING A DISCIPLE

He has told you men what is good and what it is the Lord requires of you: Only to act justly, to love faithfulness, and to walk humbly with your God.

Micah 6:8 Holman CSB

Jesus' disciples came from all walks of life: blue collar and professionals, including fishermen and a tax collector. They were from different political spectrums, including some passionate zealots. These twelve men came with diverse personalities and emotional traits: from Peter the impulsive to Thomas the doubter.

God is still in the business of acquiring disciples: ditch diggers and presidents; Republicans, Democrats, and independents; introverts and extroverts. His only criterion is that you believe in Him and be willing to sacrifice your all for His kingdom's work.

Real men and women become disciples by forsaking all and giving their lives to Christ. It is not easy, but those who stay the course are rewarded with a life of passion and purpose.

There is not Christianity without a cross, for you cannot be a disciple of Jesus without taking up your cross.

Henry Blackaby

YOUR ENCOURAGING WORDS

No rotten talk should come from your mouth, but only what is good for the building up of someone in need, in order to give grace to those who hear.

Ephesians 4:29 Holman CSB

One of the reasons that God placed you here on earth is so that you might become a beacon of encouragement to the world. As a faithful follower of the One from Galilee, you have every reason to be hopeful, and you have every reason to share your hopes with others. When you do, you will discover that hope, like other human emotions, is contagious.

As a follower of Christ, you are instructed to choose your words carefully so as to build others up through wholesome, honest encouragement (Ephesians 4:29) So look for the good in others and celebrate the good that you find. As the old saying goes, "When someone does something good, applaud—you'll make two people happy."

Encouragement starts at home, but it should never end there.

Marie T. Freeman

EXPECTATIONS

My dear friends, don't let public opinion influence how you live out our glorious, Christ-originated faith.

James 2:1 MSG

Our world is filled with pressures: some good, some bad. The pressures that we feel to behave responsibly are positive pressures. God places these pressures on our hearts, and He intends that we act accordingly. But we also face different pressures, ones that are definitely not from God.

Society seeks to mold us into more worldly beings; God seeks to mold us into new beings, more spiritual beings, beings that are most certainly not conformed to this world.

If we desire to lead responsible lives—and if we seek to please God—we must resist the pressures that society seeks to impose upon us. We must resist the temptation to do the "popular" thing, and we must insist, instead, upon doing the right thing. Period!

—TODAY'S PRAYER—

Thank You Lord, for the perfect example of how to live, Your Son, Jesus Christ. Help me follow Your voice, Father, not the multitude of voices demanding my attention. And, let me meet Your expectations for my life by serving and loving those whom You have placed along my path. Amen

HEARTS NOT TROUBLED

Peace I leave with you. My peace I give to you. I do not give to you as the world gives. Your heart must not be troubled or fearful.

John 14:27 Holman CSB

Even dedicated followers of Christ may find their courage tested by the inevitable disappointments and tragedies of life. The next time you find your courage tested, remember that God is as near as your next breath, and remember that He offers salvation to His children. He is your shield and your strength. Call upon Him in your hour of need and be comforted. Whatever the size of your challenge, God is bigger.

Fear and doubt are conquered by a faith that rejoices. And faith can rejoice because the promises of God are as certain as God Himself.

Kay Arthur

—TODAY'S PRAYER—

Your Word reminds me, Lord, that even when I walk through the valley of the shadow of death, I need fear no evil, for You are with me, and You comfort me. Thank You, Lord, for a perfect love that casts out fear. Let me live courageously and faithfully this day and every day. Amen

HE EXPECTS US TO FORGIVE

Blessed are the merciful, because they will be shown mercy.
Matthew 5:7 Holman CSB

Forgiveness is seldom easy, but it is always right. When we forgive those who have hurt us, we honor God by obeying His commandments. But when we harbor bitterness against others, we disobey God—with predictably unhappy results.

Are you easily frustrated by the inevitable shortcomings of others? Are you a prisoner of bitterness or regret? If so, perhaps you need a refresher course in the art of forgiveness.

If there exists even one person, alive or dead, whom you have not forgiven (and that includes yourself), follow God's commandment and His will for your life: forgive that person today. And remember that bitterness, anger, and regret are not part of God's plan for your life. Forgiveness is.

—TODAY'S PRAYER—

Dear Lord, sometimes forgiveness is difficult indeed. Today, Father, I ask You to help me move beyond feelings of bitterness and anger. Jesus forgave those who hurt Him; let me walk in His footsteps by forgiving those who have injured me. Amen

GIVE GENEROUSLY

You should remember the words of the Lord Jesus: "It is more blessed to give than to receive."

Acts 20:35 NLT

God's gifts are beyond description, His blessings beyond comprehension. God has been incredibly generous with us, and He rightfully expects us to be generous with others. That's why the thread of generosity is woven into the very fabric of God's teachings.

In the Old Testament, we are told that, "The good person is generous and lends lavishly..." (Psalm 112:5 MSG). And in the New Testament we are instructed, "Freely you have received, freely give" (Matthew 10:8 NKJV). These principles still apply. As we establish priorities for our days and our lives, we are advised to give freely of our time, our possessions, and our love— just as God has given freely to us.

Of course, we can never fully repay God for His gifts, but we can share them with others. And we should.

—TODAY'S PRAYER—

Lord, make me a generous and cheerful giver. Help me to give generously of my time and my possessions as I care for those in need. And, make me a humble giver, Lord, so that all the glory and the praise might be Yours. Amen

HE TEACHES

Teach me to do Your will, for You are my God. May Your gracious Spirit lead me on level ground.

Psalm 143:10 Holman CSB

God has plans for your life, but He won't force those plans upon you. To the contrary, He has given you free will, the ability to make decisions on your own. With that freedom to choose comes the responsibility of living with the consequences of the choices you make.

If you seek to live in accordance with God's will for your life—and you should—then you will live in accordance with His commandments. You will study God's Word, and you will be watchful for His signs. You will associate with fellow Christians who will encourage your spiritual growth, and you will listen to that inner voice that speaks to you in the quiet moments of your daily devotionals.

God intends to use you in wonderful, unexpected ways if you let Him. The decision to seek God's plan and to follow it is yours and yours alone. The consequences of that decision have implications that are both profound and eternal, so choose carefully.

I'm convinced that there is nothing that can happen to me in this life that is not precisely designed by a sovereign Lord to give me the opportunity to learn to know Him.

Elisabeth Elliot

DOING GOOD WORKS

Here is a simple, rule-of-thumb for behavior: Ask yourself what you want people to do for you, then grab the initiative and do it for them. Add up God's Law and Prophets and this is what you get.

Matthew 7:12 MSG

The words of Matthew 7:12 remind us that, as believers in Christ, we are commanded to treat others as we wish to be treated. This commandment is, indeed, the Golden Rule for Christians of every generation. When we weave the thread of kindness into the very fabric of our lives, we give glory to the One who gave His life for ours.

Because we are imperfect human beings, we are, on occasion, selfish, thoughtless, or cruel. But God commands us to behave otherwise. He teaches us to rise above our own imperfections and to treat others with unselfishness and love. When we observe God's Golden Rule, we help build His kingdom here on earth. And, when we share the love of Christ, we share a priceless gift; may we share it today and every day that we live.

It is one of the most beautiful compensations of life that no one can sincerely try to help another without helping herself.

Barbara Johnson

HOW LONG?

Weeping may go on all night, but joy comes with the morning.

Psalm 30:5 NLT

Once grieving begins, almost everyone wonders: "How long will it last?" There is no universal answer to this question. Different people grieve in different ways. You, therefore, will grieve at your own pace.

Mourning is a process that cannot be hurried; each significant loss is experienced and processed according to its own timetable. But in the darkness of your own particular sorrow, it is imperative to remember that God stands forever ready, offering His healing hand to you.

—TODAY'S PRAYER—

Lord, You have promised that You will not give us more than we can bear; You have promised to lift us out of our grief and despair; You have promised to put a new song on our lips. Today, Lord, I pray for those who mourn, and I thank You for sustaining all of us in our days of sorrow. May we trust You always and praise You forever. Amen

FEARING GOD

Honor all people. Love the brotherhood. Fear God. Honor the king.

1 Peter 2:17 NKJV

God's hand shapes the universe, and it shapes our lives. God maintains absolute sovereignty over His creation, and His power is beyond comprehension. As believers, we must cultivate a sincere respect for God's awesome power. God has dominion over all things, and until we acknowledge His sovereignty, we lack the humility we need to live righteously, and we lack the humility we need to become wise.

The fear of the Lord is, indeed, the beginning of knowledge. So today, as you face the realities of everyday life, remember this: until you acquire a healthy, respectful fear of God's power, your education is incomplete, and so is your faith.

The remarkable thing about fearing God is that when you fear God, you fear nothing else, whereas if you do not fear God, you fear everything else.

Oswald Chambers

MISTAKES

If we confess our sins to him, he is faithful and just to forgive us and to cleanse us from every wrong.

1 John 1:9 NLT

Every teacher who has ever graded a paper understands that the old saying is true: "To err is human…." Yes, we human beings—students and teachers alike—are inclined to make mistakes, and lots of them. When we commit the inevitable blunders of life, let us be quick to correct our errors. And, when we are hurt by the mistakes of others, let us be quick to forgive, just as God has forgiven us.

Very few things motivate us to give God our undivided attention like being faced with the negative consequences of our decisions.

Charles Stanley

—TODAY'S PRAYER—

Lord, I know that I am imperfect and that I fail You in many ways. Thank You for Your forgiveness and for Your unconditional love. Show me the error of my ways, Lord, that I might confess my wrongdoing and correct my mistakes. And, let me grow each day in wisdom, in faith, and in my love for You. Amen

PATIENCE IN THE CLASSROOM

Patience is better than pride.

Ecclesiastes 7:8 NLT

Students, even the most dedicated and well-intentioned, are far from perfect. They make mistakes and misbehave; they don't always listen, and they don't always complete their assignments. In an imperfect school filled with imperfect people, a teacher's patience is tested many times each day. But, God's instructions are clear: "be patient, bearing with one another in love" (Ephesians 4:2 NIV). As believers, we must exercise patience, even when doing so is difficult.

Psalm 37:7 commands us to, "Be still before the Lord and wait patiently for Him." But, for most of us, waiting quietly for God is difficult. Why? Because we are fallible human beings, often quick to anger and slow to forgive. Still, God instructs us to be patient in all things, and that's as it should be. After all, think how patient God has been with us.

—TODAY'S PRAYER—

Dear Lord, help me to understand the wisdom of patience. When I am hurried, slow me down. When I become impatient with others, give me empathy. Today, let me be a patient servant and a patient teacher, as I serve You and bring glory to Your Son. Amen

PRAISE PAYS

Praise the LORD. Give thanks to the LORD, for he is good; his love endures forever.

Psalm 106:1 NIV

The Bible makes it clear: it pays to praise God. But sometimes, we allow ourselves to become so preoccupied with the demands of everyday life that we forget to say "Thank You" to the Giver of all good gifts.

Worship and praise should be a part of everything we do. Otherwise, we quickly lose perspective as we fall prey to the demands of the moment.

Do you sincerely desire to be a worthy servant of the One who has given you eternal love and eternal life? Then praise Him for who He is and for what He has done for you. And don't just praise Him on Sunday morning. Praise Him all day long, every day, for as long as you live . . . and then for all eternity.

—TODAY'S PRAYER—

Dear Lord, today and every day I will praise You. I will come to You with hope in my heart and words of gratitude on my lips. Let me follow in the footsteps of Your Son, and let my thoughts, my prayers, my words, and my deeds praise You, now and forever. Amen

RELATIONSHIPS

Regarding life together and getting along with each other, you don't need me to tell you what to do. You're God-taught in these matters. Just love one another!

1 Thessalonians 4:9 MSG

As we travel along life's road, we exchange countless hugs and build lifelong relationships with a small, dear circle of family and friends. And how best do we build and maintain these relationships? Healthy relationships are built upon honesty, compassion, responsible behavior, trust, and optimism. Healthy relationships are built upon the Golden Rule. Healthy relationships are built upon sharing and caring.

Are you the kind of teacher who spends the time and the energy required to build strong, healthy, lasting relationships? Barbara Bush had this advice: "Cherish your human connections—your relationships with friends and family." And that's wise counsel because you are blessed, you are loved, and you are vitally important to your family and friends—they most certainly need you, and you most certainly need them.

Healthy relationships include laughter. Every relationship, whether it is with your spouse or your children, can be filled with joy and with laughter.

Dennis Swanberg

HERE AND NOW

The LORD is good to those whose hope is in him, to the one who seeks him.

Lamentations 3:25 NIV

Sometimes, in the crush of our daily duties, God seems far away. But He is not. God is everywhere you have ever been and everywhere you will ever go. He is with you night and day; He knows your every thought; He hears your every heartbeat. He is with you at home, and He is with you in the classroom. When you earnestly seek Him, you will find Him because He is here, waiting patiently for you to reach out to Him . . . right here . . . right now.

We are never more fulfilled than when our longing for God is met by His presence in our lives.

Billy Graham

Time spent in seeking the Holy Spirit is the most fruitful time of one's life.

E. Stanley Jones

—TODAY'S PRAYER—

How comforting it is, Dear Lord, to know that if I seek You, I will find You. You are with me, Father, every step that I take. Let me reach out to You, and let me praise You for revealing Your Word, Your way, and Your love. Amen

STEWARDSHIP

Based on the gift they have received, everyone should use it to serve others, as good managers of the varied grace of God.
1 Peter 4:10 Holman CSB

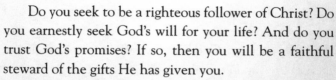

Do you seek to be a righteous follower of Christ? Do you earnestly seek God's will for your life? And do you trust God's promises? If so, then you will be a faithful steward of the gifts He has given you.

Oswald Chambers advised, "Never support an experience which does not have God as its source, and faith in God as its result." And so it is with our tithes. When we return to God that which is rightfully His, we experience the spiritual growth that always accompanies obedience to Him. But, when we attempt to shortchange our Creator, either materially or spiritually, we distance ourselves from God. The consequences of our disobedience are as predictable as they are tragic.

As Christians, we are called to walk with God and to obey His commandments. To do so is an act of holiness. God deserves our obedience. May we obey Him in all things, including our tithes.

A steward is one who manages another's resources. Each of us is a manager, not an owner. God is the owner, and we are to manage according to His plan.

Larry Burkett

THANKSGIVING

Enter his gates with thanksgiving, go into his courts with praise. Give thanks to him and bless his name.

Psalm 100:4 NLT

As believing Christians, we are blessed beyond measure. God sent His only Son to die for our sins. And, by His grace, God has given us the priceless gifts of eternal love and eternal life. We, in turn, are instructed to approach our Heavenly Father with reverence and thanksgiving. But, as busy professionals caught between the rush of everyday living and the demands of the classroom, we may sometimes fail to pause and thank our Creator for His countless blessings.

When we slow down and express our gratitude to the One who made us, we enrich our own lives and the lives of those around us. Thanksgiving should become a habit, a regular part of our daily routines. Yes, God has blessed us beyond measure, and we owe Him everything, including our eternal praise.

We ought to give thanks for all fortune: if it is good, because it is good, if bad, because it works in us patience, humility, and the contempt of this world along with the hope of our eternal country.

C. S. Lewis

WALKING WITH GOD

Are you tired? Worn out? Burned out on religion? Come to me. Get away with me and you'll recover your life. I'll show you how to take a real rest. Walk with me and work with me . . . watch how I do it. Learn the unforced rhythms of grace. I won't lay anything heavy or ill-fitting on you. Keep company with me and you'll learn to live freely and lightly.

Matthew 11:28-30 MSG

Are you discouraged? Fearful? Tired? Be comforted. Take a walk with God. Jesus called upon believers to walk with Him, and He promised them that He would teach them how to live freely and lightly (Matthew 11:28-30). Are you worried or anxious? Be confident in God's power. He will never desert you. Do you see no hope for the future? Be courageous and call upon God. He will protect you and then use you according to His purposes. Are you grieving? Know that God hears your suffering. He will comfort you and, in time, He will dry your tears. Are you confused? Listen to the quiet voice of your Heavenly Father. He is not a God of confusion. Talk with Him; listen to Him; follow His commandments. He is steadfast, and He is your Protector . . . forever.

You can't walk with God and hold hands with Satan at the same time.

Anonymous

OUR DEVINE KEEPER

This is my comfort in my affliction, for Your word has given me life.

Psalm 119:50 NKJV

Have you ever faced challenges that seemed too big to handle? Have you ever faced big problems that, despite your best efforts, simply could not be solved? If so, you know how uncomfortable it is to feel helpless in the face of difficult circumstances. Thankfully, even when there's nowhere else to turn, you can turn your thoughts and prayers to God, and He will respond.

God's hand uplifts those who turn their hearts and prayers to Him. Count yourself among that number. When you do, you can live courageously and joyfully, knowing that "this too will pass"—but that God's love for you will not. And you can draw strength from the knowledge that you are a marvelous creation, loved, protected, and uplifted by the ever-present hand of God.

—TODAY'S PRAYER—

Dear Lord, You protect me and keep me. Today, I thank You, Father, for Your love, Your protection, and Your Son. Amen

JUDGING OTHERS

Why do you look at the speck in your brother's eye, but don't notice the log in your own eye? Or how can you say to your brother, 'Let me take the speck out of your eye,' and look, there's a log in your eye? Hypocrite! First take the log out of your eye, and then you will see clearly to take the speck out of your brother's eye.

Matthew 7:3-5 Holman CSB

As teachers, we must grade our students based upon their work and their conduct. But as Christians, we must be careful that we not judge our students, or, for that matter, to condemn them when they fall short. The distinction between grading and judging is subtle but, for Christians, important. Grading students is our job; judging them is God's job.

All of us have fallen short of God's commandments, and He has forgiven us. We, too, must forgive others when they fall short. And, we must refrain from judging them.

As Christian believers, we are warned that to judge others is to invite fearful consequences: to the extent we judge others, so, too, will we be judged by God. Let us refrain, then, from judging our students, our neighbors, our family members, or our friends. Instead, let us love them and leave the judging to a far higher and far more capable authority.

GOD'S COMFORT

God, who comforts the downcast, comforted us....

2 Corinthians 7:6 NIV

The hand of God is a comforting hand. As Christians, we can be assured of this fact: Whether we find ourselves on the pinnacle of the mountain or in the darkest depths of the valley, God is there.

If you have been touched by the transforming hand of Jesus, then you have every reason to live courageously. After all, Christ has already won the ultimate battle— and He won it for you—on the cross at Calvary. Still, even if you are a dedicated Christian, you may find yourself discouraged by the inevitable disappointments and tragedies that occur in the lives of believers and non-believers alike.

The next time you find your courage tested to the limit, lean upon God's promises. Trust His Son. Remember that God is always near and that He is your protector and your deliverer. When you are worried, anxious, or afraid, call upon Him and accept the touch of His comforting hand. Remember that God rules both mountaintops and valleys—with limitless wisdom and love—now and forever.

Put your hand into the hand of God. He gives the calmness and serenity of heart and soul.

Mrs. Charles E. Cowman

ACCEPTANCE

For everything created by God is good, and nothing should be rejected if it is received with thanksgiving.

1 Timothy 4:4 Holman CSB

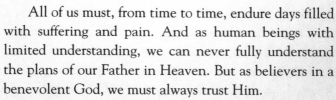

All of us must, from time to time, endure days filled with suffering and pain. And as human beings with limited understanding, we can never fully understand the plans of our Father in Heaven. But as believers in a benevolent God, we must always trust Him.

When Jesus went to the Mount of Olives, He poured out His heart to God (Luke 22). Jesus knew of the agony that He was destined to endure, but He also knew that God's will must be done.

We, like our Savior, face trials that bring fear and trembling to the very depths of our souls, but like Christ, we, too, must seek God's will, not our own. When we learn to accept God's will without reservation, we experience the peace that He offers to wise believers who trust Him completely.

—TODAY'S PRAYER—

Dear Lord, let me live in the present, not the past. Let me focus on my blessings, not my sorrows. Give me the wisdom to be thankful for the gifts that I do have, not bitter about the things that I don't have. Let me accept what was, let me give thanks for what is, and let me have faith in what most surely will be: the promise of eternal life with You. Amen

DISCOURAGED?

For God has not given us a spirit of fearfulness, but one of power, love, and sound judgment.

2 Timothy 1:7 Holman CSB

We Christians have many reasons to celebrate. God is in His heaven; Christ has risen, and we are the sheep of His flock. Yet sometimes, even the most devout Christians can become discouraged. Discouragement, however, is not God's way. He is a God of possibility not negativity. So today, let us count our blessings instead of our hardships. And, let us thank the Giver of all things good for gifts that are simply too numerous to count.

You've heard the saying, 'Life is what you make it.' That means we have a choice. We can choose to have a life full of frustration and fear, but we can just as easily choose one of joy and contentment.

Dennis Swanberg

—TODAY'S PRAYER—

Dear Lord, I pray for an attitude that pleases You. In every circumstance, I will strive to celebrate the life You have given me . . . and I will praise You for Your priceless gifts. Amen

WHAT DO YOU EXPECT?

This is the day the Lord has made; let us rejoice and be glad in it.

Psalm 118:24 Holman CSB

What do you expect from the day ahead? Are you expecting God to do wonderful things, or are you living beneath a cloud of apprehension and doubt. Do you expect God to use you in unexpected ways, or do you expect another uneventful day to pass with little fanfare? As a thoughtful believer, the answer to these questions should be obvious.

For Christians, every new day offers exciting possibilities. God's Word promises that Christ has come to this earth to give us abundant life and eternal salvation. We, in turn, should respond to God's gifts by treasuring each day and using our time here on earth to glorify our Creator and share the Good News of His Son.

Each day is a special gift from God, a treasure to be savored and celebrated. May we—as believers who have so much to celebrate—never fail to praise our Creator by rejoicing in His glorious creation.

When your life comes to a close, you will remember not days but moments. Treasure each one.

Barbara Johnson

HE LOVES US STILL

Who will separate us from the love of Christ? Will tribulation, or distress, or persecution, or famine, or nakedness, or peril, or sword? But in all these things we overwhelmingly conquer through Him who loved us.

Romans 8:35,37 NASB

Even though we are imperfect, fallible human beings, even though we have fallen far short of God's commandments, Christ loves us still. His love is perfect and steadfast; it does not waver—it does not change. Our task, as believers, is to accept Christ's love and to encourage others to do likewise.

In today's troubled world, we all need the love and the peace that is found through the Son of God. Thankfully, Christ's love has no limits; it can encircle all of us. And it's up to each of us to ensure that it does.

Christ is with us . . . and the warmth is contagious.

Joni Eareckson Tada

—TODAY'S PRAYER—

Dear Lord, I offer thanksgiving and praise for the gift of Your only begotten Son. His love is boundless, infinite, and eternal. And, as an expression of my love for Him, let me share His message with my family, with my friends, and with the world. Amen

TRUST YOUR CONSCIENCE

I always do my best to have a clear conscience toward God and men.

Acts 24:16 Holman CSB

A clear conscience is one of the many rewards you earn when you obey God's Word and follow His will. Whenever you know that you've done the right thing, you feel better about yourself, your life, and your future. A guilty conscience, on the other hand, is, for most people, it's own punishment.

In order to keep your conscience clear, you should study God's Word and obey it—you should seek God's will and follow it—you should honor God's Son and walk with Him. When you do, your earthly rewards are never-ceasing, and your heavenly rewards are everlasting.

God has revealed Himself in man's conscience. Conscience has been described as the light of the soul.

Billy Graham

—TODAY'S PRAYER—

Dear Lord, You speak to me through the gift of Your Holy Word. And, Father, You speak to me through that still small voice that tells me right from wrong. Let me follow Your way, Lord, and, in these quiet moments, show me Your plan for this day, that I might serve You. Amen

EARLY MORNING DEVOTIONS

It is good to give thanks to the Lord, to sing praises to the Most High. It is good to proclaim your unfailing love in the morning, your faithfulness in the evening.

Psalm 92:1-2 NLT

If you ever find that you're simply "too busy" for a daily chat with your Father in heaven, it's time to take a long, hard look at your priorities and your values. Each day has 1,440 minutes—do you value your relationship with God enough to spend a few of those minutes with Him? He deserves that much of your time and more—is He receiving it from you? Hopefully so.

As you consider your plans for the day ahead, here's a tip: organize your life around this simple principle: "God first." When you place your Creator where He belongs—at the very center of your day and your life—the rest of your priorities will fall into place.

Maintenance of the devotional mood is indispensable to success in the Christian life.

A. W. Tozer

—TODAY'S PRAYER—

Dear Lord, help me to hear Your direction for my life in the solitary moments that I spend with You. And as I fulfill my responsibilities throughout the day, let my actions and my thoughts be pleasing to You. Amen

QUESTIONS?

When I am filled with cares, Your comfort brings me joy.
Psalm 94:19 Holman CSB

Even the most faithful Christians are overcome by occasional bouts of fear and doubt. You are no different. When you feel that your faith is being tested to its limits, seek the comfort and assurance of the One who sent His Son as a sacrifice for you.

Have you ever felt your faith in God slipping away? If so, you are not alone. Every life—including yours—is a series of successes and failures, celebrations and disappointments, joys and sorrows, hopes and doubts.

But even when you feel very distant from God, remember that God is never distant from you. When you sincerely seek His presence, He will touch your heart, calm your fears, and restore your soul.

There is a difference between doubt and unbelief. Doubt is a matter of mind: we cannot understand what God is doing or why He is doing it. Unbelief is a matter of will: we refuse to believe God's Word and obey what He tells us to do.

Warren Wiersbe

EVIL

Be self-controlled and alert. Your enemy the devil prowls around like a roaring lion looking for someone to devour. Resist him, standing firm in the faith....

1 Peter 5:8-9 NIV

This world is God's creation, and it contains the wonderful fruits of His handiwork. But, it also contains countless opportunities to stray from God's will. Temptations are everywhere, and the devil, it seems, never takes a day off. Our task, as believers, is to turn away from temptation and to place our lives squarely in the center of God's will.

In a letter to believers, Peter offers a stern warning: "Your adversary, the devil, prowls around like a roaring lion, seeking someone to devour" (I Peter 5:8 NASB). What was true in New Testament times is equally true in our own. Satan tempts his prey and then devours them. As believing Christians, we must beware. And, if we seek righteousness in our own lives, we must earnestly wrap ourselves in the protection of God's Holy Word. When we do, we are secure.

Of two evils, choose neither.

C. H. Spurgeon

HE IS FAITHFUL

Yet faith comes from listening to this message of good news—the Good News about Christ.

Romans 10:17 NLT

When we face adversity, illness, or heartbreak, living by faith can be difficult indeed. Still, God remains faithful to us, and we should remain faithful to Him. When we do, we not only glorify the One who made us, we also serve as worthy examples to those whom we teach.

God needs no one, but when faith is present, he works through anyone.

A. W. Tozer

It's not the strength of your faith that's important. It's the object of your faith. If you are trusting God, then you will receive all that God can give you.

Warren Wiersbe

—TODAY'S PRAYER—

Dear Lord, help me to be a teacher whose faith is strong and whose heart is pure. Help me to remember that You are always near and that You can overcome any challenge. With Your love and Your power, Lord, I can live courageously and faithfully today and every day. Amen

FOCUS

Don't look for shortcuts to God. The market is flooded with surefire, easygoing formulas for a successful life that can be practiced in your spare time. Don't fall for that stuff, even though crowds of people do. The way to life—to God!—is vigorous and requires total attention.

Matthew 7:13-14 MSG

Is Christ the focus of your life? Are you fired with enthusiasm for Him? Are you an energized Christian who allows God's Son to reign over every aspect of your day? Make no mistake: that's exactly what God intends for you to do.

God has given you the gift of eternal life through His Son. In response to God's priceless gift, you are instructed to focus your thoughts, your prayers, and your energies upon God and His only begotten Son. To do so, you must resist the subtle yet powerful temptation to become a "spiritual dabbler."

A person who dabbles in the Christian faith is unwilling to place God in His rightful place: above all other things. Resist that temptation; make God the cornerstone and the touchstone of your life. When you do, He will give you all the strength and wisdom you need to live victoriously for Him.

Give me the person who says, "This one thing I do, and not these fifty things I dabble in."

D. L. Moody

FRIENDSHIPS THAT HONOR HIM

This is my command: Love one another the way I loved you. This is the very best way to love. Put your life on the line for your friends.

John 15:12-13 MSG

Some friendships help us honor God; these friendships should be nurtured. Other friendships place us in situations where we are tempted to dishonor God by disobeying His commandments; friendships that dishonor God have the potential to do us great harm.

Because we tend to become like our friends, we must choose our friends carefully. Because our friends influence us in ways that are both subtle and powerful, we must ensure that our friendships are pleasing to God. When we spend our days in the presence of godly believers, we are blessed, not only by those friends, but also by our Creator.

Do you seek to live a life that is pleasing to God? If so, you should build friendships that are pleasing to Him. When you do, your Heavenly Father will bless you and your friends with gifts that are simply too numerous to count.

Don't bypass the potential for meaningful friendships just because of differences. Explore them. Embrace them. Love them.

Luci Swindoll

YOU ARE BLESSED

If you understand what I'm telling you, act like it—and live a blessed life.

John 13:17 MSG

How has God blessed you? First and foremost, He has given you the gift of eternal life through the sacrifice of His only begotten Son, but the blessings don't stop there. Today, take time to make a partial list of the God's gifts to you: the talents, the opportunities, the possessions, and the relationships that you may, on occasion, take for granted. And then, when you've spent sufficient time listing your blessings, offer a prayer gratitude to the Giver of all things good . . . and, to the best of your ability, use your gifts for the glory of His kingdom.

—TODAY'S PRAYER—

Lord, You have given me so much, and I am thankful. Today, I seek Your blessings for my life, and I know that every good thing You give me is to be shared with others. I am blessed that I might be a blessing to those around me, Father. Let me give thanks for Your gifts . . . and let me share them. Amen

FIRST, HE LOVE US

We love Him because He first loved us.

1 John 4:19 NKJV

God loves you—His love for you is deeper and more profound than you can imagine. God's love for you is so great that He sent His only Son to this earth to die for your sins and to offer you the priceless gift of eternal life.

You must decide whether or not to accept God's gift. Will you ignore it or embrace it? Will you return it or neglect it? Will you invite Christ to dwell in the center of your heart, or will you relegate Him to a position of lesser importance? The decision is yours, and so are the consequences. So choose wisely . . . and choose today.

If you have an obedience problem, you have a love problem. Focus your attention on God's love.

Henry Blackaby

—TODAY'S PRAYER—

Lord, the Bible tells me that You are my loving Father. I thank You for Your love and for Your Son. I will praise You, I will worship You, and I will love You, Dear Lord, today, tomorrow, and forever. Amen

GOD'S SUFFICIENCY

My grace is sufficient for you, for my power is made perfect in weakness.

2 Corinthians 12:9 NIV

Of this you can be sure: the loving heart of God is sufficient to meet your needs. Whatever dangers you may face, whatever heartbreaks you must endure, God is with you, and He stands ready to comfort you and to heal you.

The Psalmist writes, "Weeping may endure for a night, but joy comes in the morning" (Psalm 30:5 NKJV). But when we are suffering, the morning may seem very far away. It is not. God promises that He is "near to those who have a broken heart" (Psalm 34:18 NKJV). In times of intense sadness, we must turn to Him, and we must encourage our friends and family members to do likewise.

If you are experiencing the intense pain of a recent loss, or if you are still mourning a loss from long ago, perhaps you are now ready to begin the next stage of your journey with God. If so, be mindful of this fact: the loving heart of God is sufficient to meet any challenge, including yours. Trust the sufficient heart of God.

Like Paul, we may bear thorns so that we can discover God's perfect sufficiency.

Beth Moore

THE CROSS

But as for me, I will never boast about anything except the cross of our Lord Jesus Christ, through whom the world has been crucified to me, and I to the world.

Galatians 6:14 Holman CSB

As we consider Christ's sacrifice on the cross, we should be profoundly humbled and profoundly grateful. And today, as we come to Christ in prayer, we should do so in a spirit of quiet, heartfelt devotion to the One who gave His life so that we might have life eternal.

He was the Son of God, but He wore a crown of thorns. He was the Savior of mankind, yet He was put to death on a roughhewn cross made of wood. He offered His healing touch to an unsaved world, and yet the same hands that had healed the sick and raised the dead were pierced with nails.

Christ humbled Himself on a cross—for you. He shed His blood—for you. He has offered to walk with you through this life and throughout all eternity. As you approach Him today in prayer, think about His sacrifice and His grace. And be humble.

The cross that Jesus commands you and me to carry is the cross of submissive obedience to the will of God, even when His will includes suffering and hardship and things we don't want to do.

Anne Graham Lotz

MANY PROMISES

This is my comfort in my affliction: Your promise has given me life.

Psalm 119:50 Holman CSB

God has made quite a few promises to you, and He intends to keep every single one of them. You will find these promises in a book like no other: the Holy Bible. The Bible is your roadmap for life here on earth and for life eternal—as a believer, you are called upon to trust its promises, to follow its commandments, and to share its Good News.

God has made promises to all of humanity and to you. God's promises never fail and they never grow old. You must trust those promises and share them with your family, with your friends, and with the world . . . starting now . . . and ending never.

We cannot rely on God's promises without obeying his commandments.

John Calvin

—TODAY'S PRAYER—

Lord, Your Holy Word contains promises, and I will trust them. I will use the Bible as my guide, and I will trust You, Lord, to speak to me through Your Holy Spirit and through Your Holy Word, this day and forever. Amen

BY GRACE

For by grace you are saved through faith, and this is not from yourselves; it is God's gift—not from works, so that no one can boast.

Ephesians 2:8-9 Holman CSB

God's grace is not earned . . . thank goodness! To earn God's love and His gift of eternal life would be far beyond the abilities of even the most righteous man or woman. Thankfully, God's grace is not an earthly reward for righteous behavior; it is a blessed spiritual gift that can be accepted by believers who dedicate themselves to God through Christ. When we accept Christ into our hearts, we are saved by His grace.

As you contemplate the day ahead, praise God for His blessings. He is the Giver of all things good. He is the Comforter, the Protector, the Teacher, and the Savior. Praise Him today and forever.

—TODAY'S PRAYER—

Lord, Your grace is a gift that cannot be earned. It is a gift that was given freely when I accepted Your Son as my personal Savior. Freely have I received Your gifts, Father. Let me freely share my gifts, my possessions, my time, my energy, and my faith. And let my words, my thoughts, my prayers, and my deeds bring honor to You and to Your Son, now and forever. Amen

HONORING GOD

If your life honors the name of Jesus, he will honor you.
2 Thessalonians 1:12 MSG

Whom will you choose to honor today? If you honor God and place Him at the center of your life, every day is a cause for celebration. But if you fail to honor your Heavenly Father, you're asking for trouble, and lots of it.

At times, your life is probably hectic, demanding, and complicated. When the demands of life leave you rushing from place to place with scarcely a moment to spare, you may fail to pause and thank your Creator for the blessings He has bestowed upon you. But that's a big mistake.

Do you sincerely seek to be a worthy servant of the One who has given you eternal love and eternal life? Then honor Him for who He is and for what He has done for you. And don't just honor Him on Sunday morning. Praise Him all day long, every day, for as long as you live . . . and then for all eternity.

Knowing God's sovereignty and unconditional love imparts a beauty to life . . . and to you.

Kay Arthur

LIFE IS A GIFT

Live full lives, full in the fullness of God. God can do anything, you know—far more than you could ever imagine or guess or request in your wildest dreams! He does it not by pushing us around but by working within us, his Spirit deeply and gently within us.

Ephesians 3:19-20 MSG

Life is God's gift to you, and He intends that you celebrate His glorious gift. If you're a teacher who treasures each day—and if you encourage your students to do the same—you will be blessed by your Father in heaven.

Christian believers face the inevitable challenges and disappointments of each day armed with the joy of Christ and the promise of salvation. So whatever this day holds for you, begin it and end it with God as your partner and Christ as your Savior. And throughout the day, give thanks to the One who created you and saved you. God's love for you is infinite. Accept it joyously and be thankful.

My story. Your story. How it is told in the end and what the story says depends on what each of us does with Jesus.

Gloria Gaither

CHRISTLIKE LOVE

Above all, love each other deeply, because love covers a multitude of sins.

1 Peter 4:8 NIV

Christ's words are unambiguous: "'Love the Lord your God with all your heart and with all your soul and with all your mind.' This is the first and greatest commandment. And the second is like it: 'Love your neighbor as yourself.' All the Law and the Prophets hang on these two commandments" (Matthew 22:37-40 NIV).

But sometimes, despite our best intentions, we fall short of God's plan for our lives when we become embittered with ourselves, with our neighbors, or most especially with our Creator.

If we are to please God, we must cleanse ourselves of the negative feelings that separate us from others and from Him. In 1 Corinthians 13, we are told that love is the foundation upon which all our relationships are to be built: our relationships with others and our relationship with our Maker.

Today and every day, may we fill our hearts with love; may we never yield to bitterness. And may we praise the Son of God who, in His infinite wisdom, made love His greatest commandment.

OBEDIENCE

This is how we are sure that we have come to know Him: by keeping His commands.

1 John 2:3 Holman CSB

As concerned teachers, we must instruct our students to obey the rules of our classroom, the rules of society, and the laws of God.

Talking about obedience is easy; living obediently is considerably harder. But, if we are to be responsible role models for our families and students, we must study God's Word and obey it.

Talking about God is easy; living by His commandments is considerably harder. But, unless we are willing to abide by God's laws, all of our righteous proclamations ring hollow. So how can we best proclaim our love for the Lord? By obeying Him. And, for further instructions, read the manual.

—TODAY'S PRAYER—

Dear Heavenly Father, You have blessed me with a love that is infinite and eternal. Let me demonstrate my love for You by obeying Your commandments. Make me a faithful servant, Father, today and throughout eternity. And, let me show my love for You by sharing Your message and Your love with others. Amen

PEACE

You, Lord, give true peace to those who depend on you, because they trust you.

Isaiah 26:3 NCV

Have you found the genuine peace that can be yours through Jesus Christ? Or are you still rushing after the illusion of "peace and happiness" that the world promises but cannot deliver?

The beautiful words of John 14:27 remind us that Jesus offers us peace, not as the world gives, but as He alone gives: "Peace I leave with you, My peace I give to you; not as the world gives do I give to you. Let not your heart be troubled, neither let it be afraid" (NKJV). Our challenge is to accept Christ's peace and then, as best we can, to share His blessings with our neighbors.

Today, as a gift to yourself, to your family, and to the world, let Christ's peace become your peace. Let Him rule your heart and your thoughts. When you do, you will partake in the peace that only He can give.

—TODAY'S PRAYER—

The world talks about peace, but only You, Lord, can give a perfect and lasting peace. True peace comes through the Prince of Peace, and sometimes His peace passes all understanding. Help me to accept His peace—and share it—this day and forever. Amen

PRAYER

Therefore I want the men in every place to pray, lifting up holy hands without anger or argument.

1 Timothy 2:8 Holman CSB

Andrew Murray observed, "Some people pray just to pray, and some people pray to know God." Your task, as maturing believer, is to pray, not out of habit or obligation, but out of a sincere desire to know your Heavenly Father. Through constant prayers, you should petition God, you should praise Him, and you seek to discover His unfolding plans for your life.

Today, reach out to the Giver of all blessings. Turn to Him for guidance and for strength. Invite Him into every corner of your day. Ask Him to teach you and to lead you. And remember that no matter what your circumstances, God is never far away; He is here . . . always right here. So pray.

—TODAY'S PRAYER—

I pray to You, my Heavenly Father, because You desire it and because I need it. Prayer not only changes things, it changes me. Help me, Lord, never to face the demands of the day without first spending time with You. Amen

REPENTANCE

If My people who are called by My name will humble themselves, and pray and seek My face, and turn from their wicked ways, then I will hear from heaven, and will forgive their sin and heal their land.

2 Chronicles 7:14 NKJV

Who among us has sinned? All of us. But, God calls upon us to turn away from sin by following His commandments. And the good news is this: When we do ask God's forgiveness and turn our hearts to Him, He forgives us absolutely and completely.

Genuine repentance requires more than simply offering God apologies for our misdeeds. Real repentance may start with feelings of sorrow and remorse, but it ends only when we turn away from the sin that has heretofore distanced us from our Creator. In truth, we offer our most meaningful apologies to God, not with our words, but with our actions. As long as we are still engaged in sin, we may be "repenting," but we have not fully "repented."

Is there an aspect of your life that is distancing you from your God? If so, ask for His forgiveness, and—just as importantly—stop sinning. Then, wrap yourself in the protection of God's Word. When you do, you will be secure.

SERVING GOD

You must choose for yourselves today whom you will serve . . .
as for me and my family, we will serve the Lord.

Joshua 24:15 NCV

How can we serve God? By sharing His message, His mercy, and His love with those who cross our paths. Everywhere we look, it seems, the needs are great, and at every turn, or so it seems, so are the temptations. Still, our challenge is clear: we must love God, obey His commandments, trust His Son, and serve His children. When we place the Lord in His rightful place—at the center of our lives—then we claim spiritual treasures that will endure forever.

There are times when we are called to love, expecting nothing in return. There are times when we are called to give money to people who will never say thanks, to forgive those who won't forgive us, to come early and stay late when no one else notices.

Max Lucado

Opportunities for service abound, and you will be surprised that when you seek God's direction, a place of suitable service will emerge where you can express your love through service.

Charles Stanley

STRESSFUL DAYS

God is our refuge and strength, a very present help in trouble.

Psalm 46:1 NKJV

Every teacher knows that stressful days are an inevitable fact of modern life. And how do we deal with the challenges of being a busy educator in a demanding, 21st-century world? By turning our days and our lives over to God. Elisabeth Elliot writes, "If my life is surrendered to God, all is well. Let me not grab it back, as though it were in peril in His hand but would be safer in mine!" May we give our lives, our hopes, and our prayers to the Father, and, by doing so, accept His will and His peace.

Satan does some of his worst work on exhausted Christians when nerves are frayed and the mind is faint.

Vance Havner

—TODAY'S PRAYER—

Dear Lord, sometimes the stresses of the day leave me tired and frustrated. Renew my energy, Father, and give me perspective and peace. Let me draw comfort and courage from Your promises, from Your love, and from Your Son. Amen

HIS SUFFICIENCY

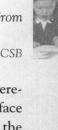

I called to the Lord in my distress; I called to my God. From His temple He heard my voice.

2 Samuel 22:7 Holman CSB

When we face the inevitable difficulties of life-here-on-earth, God stands ready to protect us. All of us face times of adversity. On occasion, we all must endure the disappointments and tragedies that befall believers and nonbelievers alike. The reassuring words of 1 John 5:4 remind us that when we accept God's grace, we overcome the passing hardships of this world by relying upon His strength, His love, and His promise of eternal life.

When we call upon God in heartfelt prayer, He will answer—in His own time and according to His own plan—and He will heal us. And while we are waiting for God's plans to unfold and for His healing touch to restore us, we can be comforted in the knowledge that our Creator can overcome any obstacle, even if we cannot. Let us take God at His Word, and let us trust Him today . . . and every day.

Crisis brings us face to face with our inadequacy and our inadequacy in turn leads us to the inexhaustible sufficiency of God.

Catherine Marshall

BLAME

Walking down the street, Jesus saw a man blind from birth. His disciples asked, "Rabbi, who sinned: this man or his parents, causing him to be born blind?" Jesus said, "You're asking the wrong question. You're looking for someone to blame. There is no such cause-effect here. Look instead for what God can do."

John 9:1-3 MSG

To blame others for our own problems is the height of futility. Yet blaming others is a favorite human pastime. Why? Because blaming is much easier than fixing, and criticizing others is so much easier than improving ourselves. So instead of solving our problems legitimately (by doing the work required to solve them) we are inclined to fret, to blame, and to criticize, while doing precious little else. When we do, our problems, quite predictably, remain unsolved.

Have you acquired the bad habit of blaming others for problems that you could or should solve yourself? If so, you are not only disobeying God's Word, you are also wasting your own precious time. So, instead of looking for someone to blame, look for something to fix, and then get busy fixing it. And as you consider your own situation, remember this: God has a way of helping those who help themselves, but He doesn't spend much time helping those who don't.

CHARACTER

Applying all diligence, in your faith supply moral excellence.
2 Peter 1:5 NASB

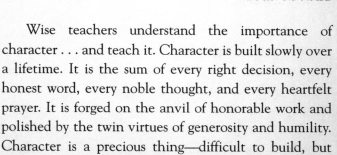

Wise teachers understand the importance of character . . . and teach it. Character is built slowly over a lifetime. It is the sum of every right decision, every honest word, every noble thought, and every heartfelt prayer. It is forged on the anvil of honorable work and polished by the twin virtues of generosity and humility. Character is a precious thing—difficult to build, but easy to tear down; godly teachers value it and protect it at all costs . . . and they encourage their students to do the same.

So many pretenders are walking around the corridors of our culture these days that genuine, sincere people wind up creating quite a stir just being themselves.

Bill Hybels

—TODAY'S PRAYER—

Heavenly Father, Your Word instructs me to walk in righteousness and in truth. Make me Your worthy servant, Lord. Let my words be true, and let my actions lead others to You. Amen

IN CHURCH

For where two or three are gathered together in My name, I am there among them.

Matthew 18:20 Holman CSB

The Bible teaches that we should worship God in our hearts and in our churches (Acts 20:28). We have clear instructions to "feed the church of God" and to worship our Creator in the presence of fellow believers.

We live in a world that is teeming with temptations and distractions—a world where good and evil struggle in a constant battle to win our minds, our hearts, and our souls. Our challenge, of course, is to ensure that we cast our lot on the side of God. One way that we remain faithful to Him is through the practice of regular, purposeful worship with our families. When we worship the Father faithfully and fervently, we are blessed.

It has always been the work of the church to bring others to belief in Christ and to experience a personal relationship with Him.

Charles Stanley

—TODAY'S PRAYER—

Dear Lord, today I pray for Your church. Let me help to feed Your flock by helping to build Your church so that others, too, might experience Your enduring love and Your eternal grace. Amen

A TAPESTRY

Be strong and courageous, and do the work. Don't be afraid or discouraged, for the Lord God, my God, is with you. He won't leave you or forsake you.

1 Chronicles 28:20 Holman CSB

Every human life, like every teaching career, is a tapestry of events: some grand, some not-so-grand, and some downright disappointing. When we reach the mountaintops of life, praising God is easy. But, when the storm clouds form overhead and we find ourselves in the dark valley of despair, our faith is stretched, sometimes to the breaking point. As Christians, we can be comforted: Wherever we find ourselves, whether at the top of the mountain or the depths of the valley, God is there, and because He cares for us, we can live courageously.

The fear of God is the death of every other fear.

C. H. Spurgeon

—TODAY'S PRAYER—

Dear Lord, sometimes I face disappointments and challenges that leave me worried and afraid. When I am fearful, let me seek Your strength. When I am anxious, give me faith. Keep me mindful, Lord, that You are my God. With You by my side, Lord, I have nothing to fear. Help me to be Your grateful and courageous servant this day and every day. Amen

IRRITATED?

A person with great anger bears the penalty; if you rescue him, you'll have to do it again.

Proverbs 19:19 Holman CSB

Sometimes, people can be discourteous and cruel. Sometimes people can be unfair, unkind, and unappreciative. Sometimes people get angry and frustrated. So what's a Christian to do? God's answer is straightforward: forgive, forget, and move on. In Luke 6:37, Jesus instructs, "Do not judge, and you will not be judged. Do not condemn, and you will not be condemned. Forgive, and you will be forgiven" (Holman CSB).

Today and every day, make sure that you're quick to forgive others for their shortcomings. And when other people misbehave (as they most certainly will from time to time), don't pay too much attention. Just forgive those people as quickly as you can, and try to move on . . . as quickly as you can.

You can be sure you are abiding in Christ if you are able to have a Christlike love toward the people that irritate you the most.

Vonette Bright

ENCOURAGE EACH OTHER

Finally, brothers, rejoice. Be restored, be encouraged, be of the same mind, be at peace, and the God of love and peace will be with you.

2 Corinthians 13:11 Holman CSB

Do you delight in the victories of others? You should. Each day provides countless opportunities to encourage others and to praise their good works. When you do so, you not only spread seeds of joy and happiness, you also obey the commandments of God's Holy Word.

Life is a team sport, and all of us need occasional pats on the back from our teammates. As Christians, we are called upon to spread the Good News of Christ, and we are also called to spread a message of encouragement and hope to the world.

Today, let us be cheerful Christians with smiles on our faces and encouraging words on our lips. By blessing others, we also bless ourselves, and, at the same time, we do honor to the One who gave His life for us.

Encouraging others means helping people, looking for the best in them, and trying to bring out their positive qualities.

John Maxwell

YOUR EXAMPLE

Set an example of good works yourself, with integrity and dignity in your teaching.

Titus 2:7 Holman CSB

What kind of example are you? Are you the kind of teacher whose life serves as a powerful example of righteousness? Are you a teacher whose behavior serves as a positive role model for students? Are you the kind of teacher whose actions, day in and day out, are based upon integrity, fidelity, and a love for the Lord? If so, you are not only blessed by God, you are also a powerful force for good in a world that desperately needs positive influences such as yours.

Phillips Brooks advised, "Be such a man, and live such a life, that if every man were such as you, and every life a life like yours, this earth would be God's Paradise." And that's sound advice.

A man ought to live so that everybody knows he is a Christian, and most of all, his family ought to know.

D. L. Moody

—TODAY'S PRAYER—

Lord, let me be a righteous example to my students. Let me be honest and good, patient and kind, faithful to You and loving to others . . . now and forever. Amen

BELONGING TO HIM

He said to him, "You shall love the Lord your God with all your heart, with all your soul, and with all your mind. This is the greatest and most important commandment.

Matthew 22:37-38 Holman CSB

If you want to know God in a more meaningful way, you need to open up your heart and let Him in.

C. S. Lewis observed, "A person's spiritual health is exactly proportional to his love for God." If you hope to receive a full measure of God's spiritual blessings, you must invite your Creator to rule over your heart. When you honor God in this way, His love expands to fill your heart and bless your life.

St. Augustine wrote, "I love you, Lord, not doubtingly, but with absolute certainty. Your Word beat upon my heart until I fell in love with you, and now the universe and everything in it tells me to love you."

Today, open your heart to the Father. And let your obedience be a fitting response to His never-ending love.

—TODAY'S PRAYER—

Heavenly Father, I am Yours. Use me in ways that accomplish Your purpose as I share the Good News of Your Son, today and every day. Amen

FORGIVENESS

See to it that no one repays evil for evil to anyone, but always pursue what is good for one another and for all.

1 Thessalonians 5:15 Holman CSB

There's no doubt about it: forgiveness is difficult. Being frail, fallible, imperfect human beings, we are quick to anger, quick to blame, slow to forgive, and even slower to forget. Yet as Christians, we are commanded to forgive others, just as we, too, have been forgiven. So even when forgiveness is difficult, we must ask God to help us move beyond the spiritual stumbling blocks of bitterness and hate.

If, in your heart, you hold bitterness against even a single person, forgive. If there exists even one person, alive or dead, whom you have not forgiven, follow God's commandment and His will for your life: forgive. If you are embittered against yourself for some past mistake or shortcoming, forgive. Then, to the best of your abilities, forget. And move on. Bitterness and regret are not part of God's plan for your life. Forgiveness is.

Forgiveness enables you to bury your grudge in icy earth. To put the past behind you. To flush resentment away by being the first to forgive. Forgiveness fashions your future. It is a brave and brash thing to do.

Barbara Johnson

THE FUTURE

Wisdom is pleasing to you. If you find it, you have hope for the future.

Proverbs 24:14 NCV

In these uncertain times, it's easy to lose hope for the future . . . but it's wrong. God instructs us to trust His wisdom, His plan, and His love. When we do so, the future becomes a glorious opportunity to help others, to praise our Creator, and to share God's Good News.

Do you have faith in the ultimate goodness of God's plan? You should. And, do you have faith in the abundant opportunities that await your students? Hopefully, you do. After all, the confidence that you display in your students can be contagious. Your belief in them can have a profound impact on the way they view themselves and their world.

Today, as you stand before your classroom, help your students face the future with optimism, hope, and self-confidence. After all, even in these uncertain times, God still has the last word. And His love endures to all generations, including this one.

The future lies all before us. Shall it only be a slight advance upon what we usually do? Ought it not to be a bound, a leap forward to altitudes of endeavor and success undreamed of before?

Annie Armstrong

GOD'S PLANS

But as it is written: What no eye has seen and no ear has heard, and what has never come into a man's heart, is what God has prepared for those who love Him.

1 Corinthians 2:9 Holman CSB

God has plans for your life and for the lives of your students. Big plans. But He won't force His plans upon you. To the contrary, He has given all of His children free will (a fact that is not lost on any teacher who has ever tried to quiet an unruly classroom). While you, as a concerned teacher, can encourage your students to seek purpose and meaning for their own lives, you can't force them to do so. You can, however, seek to discover God's plan for your life. God is listening and waiting for You to reach out to Him, and He intends to use you in wonderful, unexpected ways. So let Him.

God has no problems, only plans. There is never panic in heaven.

Corrie ten Boom

—TODAY'S PRAYER—

Dear Lord, I am Your creation, and You created me for a reason. Give me the wisdom to follow Your direction for my life's journey. Let me do Your work here on earth by seeking Your will and living it, knowing that when I trust in You, Father, I am eternally blessed. Amen

HIS GOLDEN RULE

See that no one pays back evil for evil, but always try to do good to each other and to everyone else.

1 Thessalonians 5:15 NLT

Would you like to improve your classroom and your world? If so, you can start by practicing the Golden Rule.

Jesus said, "Do to others what you want them to do to you" (Mathew 7:12 NCV). That means that you should treat everyone (including your students) in the very same way that you want to be treated.

Is the Golden Rule your rule both inside and outside the classroom? Hopefully so. After all, Jesus made Himself perfectly clear: He instructed you to treat other people in the same way that you want to be treated—no exceptions.

So if you want to know how to respond to others, ask the person you see every time you look into the mirror. It's the decent way to teach and the decent way to live.

Good will is written into the constitution of things; ill will is sand in the machinery.

E. Stanley Jones

A HAPPY HEART

A happy heart is like good medicine.

Proverbs 17:22 NCV

Do you seek happiness, abundance, and contentment? If so, here are some things you should do: Love God and His Son; depend upon God for strength; try, to the best of your abilities, to follow God's will; and strive to obey His Holy Word. When you do these things, you'll discover that happiness goes hand-in-hand with righteousness. The happiest people are not those who rebel against God; the happiest people are those who love God and obey His commandments.

What does life have in store for you? A world full of possibilities (of course it's up to you to seize them), and God's promise of abundance (of course it's up to you to accept it). So, as you embark upon the next phase of your journey, remember to celebrate the life that God has given you. Your Creator has blessed you beyond measure. Honor Him with your prayers, your words, your deeds, and your joy.

True happiness and contentment cannot come form the things of this world. The blessedness of true joy is a free gift that comes only from our Lord and Savior, Jesus Christ.

Dennis Swanberg

OUR TEACHER

The next day John saw Jesus coming toward him and said, "Here is the Lamb of God, who takes away the sin of the world!

John 1:29 Holman CSB

God sent His Son to teach mankind the path to abundance, peace, joy, and eternal life. God desires to guide you and teach you every day of your life—and of course you should be willing to accept God's instruction. But sometimes, you will be tempted to do otherwise.

Our 21st-Century world is a noisy, distracting place filled with countless opportunities to stray from God's will. The world seems to cry, "Worship me with your time, your money, your energy, and your thoughts!" But God commands otherwise: He commands us to worship Him and Him alone; everything else must be secondary.

Whenever we stray from God's commandments, we invite bitter consequences. But, when we follow His commandments—and when we genuinely and humbly seek His instruction—God touches our hearts and leads us on the path of His choosing.

Will you trust God to teach you "in the way you should go?" Prayerfully, you will, because to do otherwise is not only the opposite of wisdom; it is also the prelude to disaster.

MIRACLES

Is anything impossible for the Lord?

Genesis 18:14 Holman CSB

When, at the age of two, she was stricken with what 19th-century doctors called "brain fever," Helen Keller was left deaf and blind. Keller might have been excused for having a sour attitude about life, but she did not give in to the paralysis of bitterness and despair. Instead, with the help of an extraordinary teacher named Anne Sullivan, young Helen learned to communicate and quickly embraced education.

Eventually, Keller graduated cum laude with a degree from Radcliffe, and then went on to become a noted American writer and lecturer. She once observed, "When we do the best we can, we never know what miracles await."

What miracles await you? Big ones! When you do your part, God will do His part, and the results will be . . . miraculous!

—TODAY'S PRAYER—

Dear God, nothing is impossible for You. Your infinite power is beyond human understanding—keep me always mindful of Your strength. When I lose hope, give me faith; when others lose hope, let me teach of Your glory and Your works. Today, Lord, let me expect the miraculous, and let me trust in You. Amen

THE PAST

The Lord says, "Forget what happened before, and do not think about the past. Look at the new thing I am going to do. It is already happening. Don't you see it? I will make a road in the desert and rivers in the dry land."

Isaiah 43:18-19 NCV

When you find the courage to accept the past by forgiving all those who have injured you (including yourself), you can then look to the future with a sense of optimism and hope.

Because we are saved by a risen Christ, we can have hope for the future, no matter how troublesome our circumstances may seem. After all, God has promised that we are His throughout eternity. And, He has told us that we must place our hopes in Him.

Of course, we will face disappointments and failures while we are here on earth, but these are only temporary defeats. Of course, this world can be a place of trials and tribulations, but we are secure. God has promised us peace, joy, and eternal life. And God keeps His promises today, tomorrow, and forever.

Don't let yesterday use up too much of today.

Dennis Swanberg

PLEASING GOD

Obviously, I'm not trying to be a people pleaser! No, I am trying to please God. If I were still trying to please people, I would not be Christ's servant.

Galatians 1:10 NLT

When God created you, He equipped you with an assortment of talents and abilities that are uniquely yours. It's up to you to discover those talents and to use them, but the world may encourage you to do otherwise. At times, society will attempt to pigeonhole you, to standardize you, and to make you fit into particular, preformed mold. Perhaps God has other plans.

At times, because you're an imperfect human being, you may become so wrapped up in meeting society's expectations that you fail to focus on God's expectations.

Whom will you try to please today: God or society? Your primary obligation is not to please imperfect men and women. Your obligation is to strive diligently to meet the expectations of an all-knowing and perfect God. Period.

Make God's will the focus of your life day by day. If you seek to please Him and Him alone, you'll find yourself satisfied with life.

Kay Arthur

QUESTIONS

We are pressured in every way but not crushed; we are perplexed but not in despair.

2 Corinthians 4:8 Holman CSB

When you have a question that you simply can't answer, whom do you ask? When you face a difficult decision, to whom do you turn for counsel? To friends? To mentors? To family members? Or do you turn first to the Ultimate source of wisdom? The answers to life's Big Questions start with God and with the teachings of His Holy Word.

God's wisdom stands forever. God's Word is a light for every generation. Make it your light as well. Use the Bible as a compass for the next stage of your life's journey. Use it as the yardstick by which your behavior is measured. And as you carefully consult the pages of God's Word, prayerfully ask Him to reveal the wisdom that you need. When you take your concerns to God, He will not turn you away; He will, instead, offer answers that are tested and true. Your job is to ask, to listen, and to trust.

When there is perplexity, there is always guidance— not always at the moment we ask, but in good time, which is God's time. There is no need to fret and stew.

Elisabeth Elliot

PROCLAIM HIS SALVATION

Sing to the Lord, all the earth. Proclaim His salvation from day to day.

1 Chronicles 16:23 Holman CSB

The heart of God is a saving heart. The familiar words of John 3:16 remind us of a profound truth: God loves each of us so much that He sent His Son to die for our sins.

Your Heavenly Father offers you the priceless gift of eternal life. How will you respond? Christ sacrificed His life on the cross so that you might be with Him throughout eternity. This gift, freely given from God's only begotten Son, is a priceless possession, a treasure beyond price, yet it is freely offered to you.

God is waiting patiently for each of us to accept the gift of eternal life. Let us claim Christ's gift today. Let us walk with the Savior; let us love Him; let us praise Him; and let us share His message of salvation with the world.

There is no one so far lost that Jesus cannot find him and cannot save him.

Andrew Murray

CHOOSING YOUR WORDS

Watch the way you talk. Let nothing foul or dirty come out of your mouth. Say only what helps, each word a gift.

Ephesians 4:29 MSG

The Bible reminds us that "Reckless words pierce like a sword, but the tongue of the wise brings healing" (Proverbs 12:18 NIV). In other words, if we are to solve more problems that we start, we must measure our words carefully.

Sometimes, even the most thoughtful teachers may speak first and think second (with decidedly mixed results). A far better strategy, of course, is to do the more difficult thing: to think first and to speak next.

Do you seek to be a source of encouragement to your students? If so, you must speak words that are worthy of your Savior. So avoid angry outbursts. Refrain from impulsive outpourings. Terminate tantrums. Instead, speak words of encouragement and hope to a world that desperately needs both.

—TODAY'S PRAYER—

Lord, You have commanded me to choose my words carefully so that I might be a source of encouragement and hope to all whom I meet. Keep me mindful, Father, that I have influence on many people, especially my students . . . make me an influence for good. Amen

TAKE COURAGE

They do not fear bad news; they confidently trust the Lord to care for them. They are confident and fearless and can face their foes triumphantly.

Psalm 112:7-8 NLT

In times of adversity, we are wise to remember the words of Jesus, who, when He walked on the waters, reassured His disciples, saying, "Take courage! It is I. Don't be afraid" (Matthew 14:27 NIV). Then, with Christ on His throne and His love in our hearts, we can offer comfort to others and, by doing so, help them face their own fears with courage, determination, and faith.

Trial and triumph are what God uses to scribble all over the pages of our lives. They are signs that He is using us, loving us, shaping us to His image, enjoying our companionship, delivering us from evil, and writing eternity into our hearts.

Barbara Johnson

God has given us His promises to assure us and encourage us in the dark days of life.

Warren Wiersbe

TRUTH

Then you will know the truth, and the truth will set you free.

John 8:32 NIV

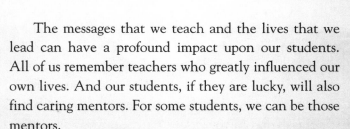

The messages that we teach and the lives that we lead can have a profound impact upon our students. All of us remember teachers who greatly influenced our own lives. And our students, if they are lucky, will also find caring mentors. For some students, we can be those mentors.

As teachers, we are in positions of leadership, and we must ensure that the messages we share with our students are sound, practical, and true. The ultimate truth, of course, is found in the Word of God through the person of His Son, Jesus. And even if Bible teachings are not a formal part of a school's curriculum, God's Word should be firmly planted in the heart of every Christian who teaches there.

As we stand before our students each day, we teach not only "what we know" but also "who we are." And make no mistake: our students will see us for who we really are and what we really believe. Let us teach—and live—accordingly.

Peace, if possible, but truth at any rate.

Martin Luther

A GENTLE ANSWER

A gentle answer turns away anger, but a harsh word stirs up wrath.

Proverbs 15:1 Holman CSB

When you allow yourself to become angry, you are certain to defeat at least one person: yourself. When you allow the minor frustrations of everyday life—or those occasional conundrums that accompany life in the classroom—to hijack your emotions, you do harm to yourself and to your loved ones. So today and every day, guard yourself against the kind of angry thinking that inevitably takes a toll on your emotions and your relationships. It's the wise way to live and the wise way to teach.

Life is too short to spend it being angry, bored, or dull.

Barbara Johnson

—TODAY'S PRAYER—

Lord, sometimes, in moments of frustration, I become angry. When I fall prey to pettiness, restore my sense of perspective. When I fall prey to irrational anger, give me inner calm. Let me show my thankfulness to You by offering forgiveness to others. And, when I do, may others see Your love reflected through my words and my deeds. Amen

INSTRUCTIONS

Therefore, God's chosen ones, holy and loved, put on heartfelt compassion, kindness, humility, gentleness, and patience.
Colossians 3:12 Holman CSB

The instructions of Colossians 3:12 are unambiguous: as Christians, we are to be compassionate, humble, gentle, and kind. But sometimes, we fall short. In the busyness and confusion of daily life, we may neglect to share a kind word or a kind deed. This oversight hurts others, but it hurts us most of all.

Today, slow yourself down and be alert for those who need your smile, your kind words, or your helping hand. Make kindness a centerpiece of your dealings with others. They will be blessed, and you will be too. Today, honor Christ by obeying His Golden Rule. He expects no less, and He deserves no less.

—TODAY'S PRAYER—

Lord, sometimes this world can become a place of busyness, frustration, and confusion. Slow me down, Lord, that I might see the needs of those around me. Today, help me show mercy to those in need. Today, let me spread kind words of thanksgiving and celebration in honor of Your Son. Today, let forgiveness rule my heart. And every day, Lord, let my love for Christ be reflected through deeds of kindness for those who need the healing touch of the Master's hand. Amen

PATIENCE AND MORE PATIENCE

He has made everything appropriate in its time. He has also put eternity in their hearts, but man cannot discover the work God has done from beginning to end.

Ecclesiastes 3:11 Holman CSB

Students, as a whole, can be quite an impatient lot. They can't wait for class to end; ditto for the school day and the school week. They wait impatiently for Christmas vacation, spring break, and—most urgently—summer vacation. But, wise teachers understand that life beyond the classroom requires patience, patience, and more patience. Unlike the precisely charted school year, life unfolds according to a timetable that is ordained, not by man, but by God. Let us, as believers, wait patiently for God. And let us teach patience to those who look to us for guidance . . . even if they're squirming in their seats, waiting for the bell to ring.

—TODAY'S PRAYER—

Dear Lord, Your timing is seldom my timing, but Your timing is always right for me. You are my Father, and You have a plan for my life that is grander than I can imagine. When I am impatient, remind me that You are never early or late. You are always on time, Lord, so let me trust in You . . . always. Amen

BELONGING TO HIM

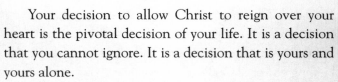

Therefore if anyone is in Christ, he is a new creature; the old things passed away; behold, new things have come.

2 Corinthians 5:17 Holman CSB

Your decision to allow Christ to reign over your heart is the pivotal decision of your life. It is a decision that you cannot ignore. It is a decision that is yours and yours alone.

God's love for you is deeper and more profound than you can imagine. God's love for you is so great that He sent His only Son to this earth to die for your sins and to offer you the priceless gift of eternal life. Now, you must decide whether or not to accept God's gift. Will you ignore it or embrace it? Will you return it or neglect it? Will you accept Christ's love and build a lifelong relationship with Him, or will you turn away from Him and take a different path?

Accept God's gift now: allow His Son to preside over your heart, your thoughts, and your life, starting this very instant.

Jesus is the personal approach from the unseen God coming so near that he becomes inescapable. You don't have to find him—you just have to consent to be found.

E. Stanley Jones

ASKING GOD

You do not have because you do not ask.

James 4:2 Holman CSB

Are you in need? Ask God to sustain you. Are you troubled? Take your worries to Him in prayer. Are you weary? Seek God's strength. In all things great and small—inside the classroom and outside it—seek the healing power of God's grace. He hears your prayers, and He will answer.

When you ask God to do something, don't ask timidly; put your whole heart into it.

Marie T. Freeman

Don't be afraid to ask your heavenly Father for anything you need. Indeed, nothing is too small for God's attention or too great for his power.

Dennis Swanberg

—TODAY'S PRAYER—

Lord, You are the giver of all things good. When I am in need, let me come to You in prayer. You know the desires of my heart, Lord; grant them, I ask. Yet not my will, Father, but Your will be done. Amen

CELEBRATE YOUR LIFE

David and the whole house of Israel were celebrating before the Lord.

2 Samuel 6:5 Holman CSB

God gives us this day; He fills it to the brim with possibilities, and He challenges us to use it for His purposes. The 118th Psalm reminds us that today, like every other day, is a cause for celebration. The day is presented to us fresh and clean at midnight, free of charge, but we must beware: Today is a non-renewable resource—once it's gone, it's gone forever. Our responsibility, of course, is to use this day in the service of God's will and according to His commandments.

Today, treasure the time that God has given you. Give Him the glory and the praise and the thanksgiving that He deserves. And search for the hidden possibilities that God has placed along your path. This day is a priceless gift from God, so use it joyfully and encourage others to do likewise. After all, this is the day the Lord has made.

Some of us seem so anxious about avoiding hell that we forget to celebrate our journey toward heaven.

Philip Yancey

EMPTY?

Then He said to them all, "If anyone wants to come with Me, he must deny himself, take up his cross daily, and follow Me."

Luke 9:23 Holman CSB

Even the most inspired Christian teachers can, from time to time, find themselves running on empty. The demands of daily life combined with the stresses of the classroom can drain us of our strength and rob us of the joy that is rightfully ours in Christ.

God's Word is clear: When we genuinely lift our hearts and prayers to Him, He renews our strength. Are you almost too weary to lift your head? Then bow it. Offer your concerns and your needs to your Father in Heaven. He is always at your side, offering His love and His strength.

Are you spiritually depleted? Call upon fellow believers to support you, and call upon Christ to renew your spirit and your life. When you do, you'll discover that the Creator of the universe stands always ready and always able to create a new sense of wonderment and joy in you.

Think of this—we may live together with Him here and now, a daily walking with Him who loved us and gave Himself for us.

Elisabeth Elliot

TEMPTED TO COMPLAIN?

Do everything without grumbling and arguing, so that you may be blameless and pure.

Philippians 2:14-15 Holman CSB

Because we are imperfect human beings, we often lose sight of our blessings. Ironically, most of us have more blessings than we can count, but we may still find reasons to complain about the minor frustrations of everyday life. To do so, of course, is not only wrong; it is also the pinnacle of shortsightedness and a serious roadblock on the path to spiritual abundance.

Are you tempted to complain about the inevitable minor frustrations of everyday living? Don't do it! Today and every day, make it a practice to count your blessings, not your hardships. It's the truly decent way to live.

It's your choice: you can either count your blessings or recount your disappointments.

Jim Gallery

And, at the bottom, all complainings mean just this: that we do not believe in God, and that we do not trust in His salvation.

Hannah Whitall Smith

TEACHING DISCIPLINE

Guide the young men to live disciplined lives. But mostly, show them all this by doing it yourself, incorruptible in your teaching, your words solid and sane.

Titus 2:6-8 MSG

As leaders of the classroom, we are charged with teaching discipline and, on occasion, dispensing it. We do so in the hopes that our students will learn that disciplined behavior is at the very foundation of successful living.

Those who study the Bible are confronted again and again with God's intention that His children (of all ages) lead disciplined lives. God doesn't reward laziness or misbehavior. To the contrary, He expects His own to adopt a disciplined approach to their lives, and He punishes those who disobey His commandments.

Wise teachers demonstrate the importance of discipline by their words and by their actions. Wise students pay attention . . . and learn.

—TODAY'S PRAYER—

Dear Lord, Your Holy Word tells us that You expect Your children to be diligent and disciplined. You have told us that the fields are ripe and the workers are few. Lead me to Your fields, Lord, and make me a disciplined teacher in the service of Your Son, Christ Jesus. Amen

ENTHUSIASM

Do your work with enthusiasm. Work as if you were serving the Lord, not as if you were serving only men and women.

Ephesians 6:7 NCV

John Wesley advised, "Catch on fire with enthusiasm and people will come for miles to watch you burn." His words still ring true. When we fan the flames of enthusiasm for Christ, our faith serves as a beacon to others.

Our world desperately needs faithful believers who share the Good News of Jesus with joyful exuberance. Be such a believer. The world desperately needs your enthusiasm, and just as importantly, you need the experience of sharing it.

Wherever you are, be all there. Live to the hilt every situation you believe to be the will of God.

Jim Elliot

Success or failure can be pretty well predicted by the degree to which the heart is fully in it.

John Eldredge

—TODAY'S PRAYER—

Dear Lord, let me be an enthusiastic participant in life. And let my enthusiasm bring honor and glory to You. Amen

FAITH AND ENDURANCE

Let us lay aside every weight and the sin that so easily ensnares us, and run with endurance the race that lies before us, keeping our eyes on Jesus, the source and perfecter of our faith.

Hebrews 12:1-2 Holman CSB

If heaven is such a wonderful place (and it is!), why doesn't God simply take us there when we become believers? The answer is simple: We still have work to do. And an important part of that work involves our faith—building it and sharing it.

When a suffering woman sought healing by merely touching the hem of His cloak, Jesus replied, "Daughter, be of good comfort; thy faith hath made thee whole" (Matthew 9:22 KJV). The message to believers of every generation is clear: we must live by faith today and every day.

How can you strengthen your faith? Through praise, through worship, through Bible study, and through prayer. And, as your faith becomes stronger, you will find ways to share it with your friends, your family, and with the world . . . and that, by the way, is exactly what God wants you to do.

Faith expects from God what is beyond all expectation.

Andrew Murray

FELLOWSHIP

Now finally, all of you should be like-minded and sympathetic, should love believers, and be compassionate and humble.

1 Peter 3:8 Holman CSB

Fellowship with other believers should be an integral part of your everyday life. Your association with fellow Christians should be uplifting, enlightening, encouraging, and consistent.

Are you an active member of your own fellowship? Are you a builder of bridges inside the four walls of your church and outside it? Do you contribute to God's glory by contributing your time and your talents to a close-knit band of believers? Hopefully so. The fellowship of believers is intended to be a powerful tool for spreading God's Good News and uplifting His children. And God intends for you to be a fully contributing member of that fellowship. Your intentions should be the same.

—TODAY'S PRAYER—

Heavenly Father, You have given me a community of supporters called the church. Let our fellowship be a refection of the love we feel for each other and the love we feel for You. Amen

HOW OFTEN?

Then Peter came to Him and said, "Lord, how many times could my brother sin against me and I forgive him? As many as seven times?" "I tell you, not as many as seven," Jesus said to him, "but 70 times seven."

Matthew 18:21-22 Holman CSB

How often should we forgive other people? More times than we can count. That's a mighty tall order, but we must remember that it's an order from God—an order that must be obeyed.

In God's curriculum, forgiveness isn't optional; it's a required course. Sometimes, of course, we have a very difficult time forgiving the people who have hurt us, but if we don't find it in our hearts to forgive them, we not only hurt ourselves, we also disobey our Father in heaven. So we must forgive—and keep forgiving—as long as we live.

God forgets the past. Imitate him.

Max Lucado

—TODAY'S PRAYER—

Dear Lord, Your ability to forgive is limitless; mine is not. Keep me mindful of Your commandment to forgive others—and to keep forgiving them—just as I have been forgiven by You. Amen

AN ARRAY OF TALENTS

Based on the gift they have received, everyone should use it to serve others, as good managers of the varied grace of God.
1 Peter 4:10 Holman CSB

Face it: you've got an array of talents that need to be refined. All people possess special gifts—bestowed from the Father above—and you are no exception. But, your gift is no guarantee of success; it must be cultivated—by you—or it will go unused . . . and God's gift to you will be squandered.

Today, make a promise to yourself that you will earnestly seek to discover the talents that God has given you. Then, nourish those talents and make them grow. Finally, vow to share your gifts with the world for as long as God gives you the power to do so. After all, the best way to say "Thank You" for God's gifts is to use them.

—TODAY'S PRAYER—

Lord, I praise You for Your priceless gifts. I give thanks for Your creation, for Your Son, and for the unique talents and opportunities that You have given me. Let me use my gifts for the glory of Your kingdom, this day and every day. Amen

GOD'S COMMANDMENTS

I delight in Your commands, which I love.

Psalm 119:47 Holman CSB

Since God created Adam and Eve, we human beings have been rebelling against our Creator. Why? Because we are unwilling to trust God's Word, and we are unwilling to follow His commandments. God has given us a guidebook for righteous living called the Holy Bible. It contains thorough instructions which, if followed, lead to fulfillment, righteousness, and salvation. But, if we choose to ignore God's commandments, the results are as predictable as they are tragic.

Talking about God is easy; living by His commandments is considerably harder. But, unless we are willing to abide by God's laws, all of our righteous proclamations ring hollow. How can we best proclaim our love for the Lord? By obeying Him. And, for further instructions, read the manual.

Faith, as Paul saw it, was a living, flaming thing leading to surrender and obedience to the commandments of Christ.

A. W. Tozer

CHEERFULNESS

A cheerful heart has a continual feast.

Proverbs 15:15 Holman CSB

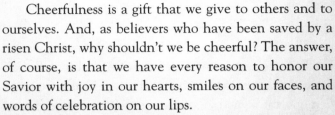

Cheerfulness is a gift that we give to others and to ourselves. And, as believers who have been saved by a risen Christ, why shouldn't we be cheerful? The answer, of course, is that we have every reason to honor our Savior with joy in our hearts, smiles on our faces, and words of celebration on our lips.

Few things in life are more sad, or, for that matter, more absurd, than grumpy Christians. Christ promises us lives of abundance and joy if we accept His love and His grace. Yet sometimes, even the most righteous among us are beset by fits of ill temper and frustration. During these moments, we may not feel like turning our thoughts and prayers to Christ, but if we seek to gain perspective and peace, that's precisely what we must do.

Are you a cheerful Christian? You should be! And what is the best way to attain the joy that is rightfully yours? By giving Christ what is rightfully His: your heart, your soul, and your life.

Christ can put a spring in your step and a thrill in your heart. Optimism and cheerfulness are products of knowing Christ.

Billy Graham

COMMUNICATION

A wise person gets known for insight; gracious words add to one's reputation...They make a lot of sense, these wise folks; whenever they speak, their reputation increases.

Proverbs 16:21,23 MSG

Think . . . pause . . . then speak: How wise is the teacher who can communicate in this fashion! But all too often, in the rush to have ourselves heard, we speak first and think next . . . with unfortunate results. Today, seek to encourage all who cross your path. Measure your words carefully. Speak wisely, not impulsively. Your words will bring healing and comfort to a world that needs both.

Attitude and the spirit in which we communicate are as important as the words we say.

Charles Stanley

Fill the heart with the love of Christ so that only truth and purity can come out of the mouth.

Warren Wiersbe

—TODAY'S PRAYER—

Dear Lord, help me speak words that are pleasing to You and helpful to Your children. Today and every day, let my words and my actions demonstrate what it means to be a faithful follower of Your Son. Amen

HAVE COURAGE

I am able to do all things through Him who strengthens me.
Philippians 4:13 Holman CSB

Because we are saved by a risen Christ, we can have hope for the future, no matter how desperate our circumstances may seem. After all, God has promised that we are His throughout eternity. And, He has told us that we must place our hopes in Him.

Today, summon the courage to follow God. Even if the path seems difficult, even if your heart is fearful, trust your Heavenly Father and follow Him. Trust Him with your day and your life. Do His work, care for His children, and share His Good News. Let Him guide your steps. He will not lead you astray.

One of the main missions of God is to free us from the debilitating bonds of fear and anxiety. God's heart is broken when He sees us so demoralized and weighed down by fear.

Bill Hybels

God shields us from most of the things we fear, but when He chooses not to shield us, He unfailingly allots grace in the measure needed.

Elisabeth Elliot

DISCIPLESHIP

Follow Me, Jesus told them, "and I will make you into fishers of men!" Immediately they left their nets and followed Him.
Mark 1:17-18 Holman CSB

When Jesus addressed His disciples, He warned that each one must, "take up his cross and follow me." The disciples must have known exactly what the Master meant. In Jesus' day, prisoners were forced to carry their own crosses to the location where they would be put to death. Thus, Christ's message was clear: in order to follow Him, Christ's disciples must deny themselves and, instead, trust Him completely. Nothing has changed since then.

If we are to be disciples of Christ, we must trust Him and place Him at very center of our beings. Jesus never comes "next." He is always first. The paradox, of course, is that only by sacrificing ourselves to Him do we gain salvation for ourselves.

Do you seek to be a worthy disciple of Christ? Then pick up His cross today and every day that you live. When you do, He will bless you now and forever.

Discipleship is a decision to live by what I know about God, not by what I feel about him or myself or my neighbors.

Eugene Peterson

SHEPHERD THE FLOCK

Shepherd the flock of God which is among you.

1 Peter 5:2 NKJV

In the classroom, we encounter a specific category of people who desperately need our encouraging words: those people are called students—all students. And, as dedicated teachers, we must find creative ways to encourage them.

Today's world can be a difficult and uncertain place, especially for young people. Many of our students are in desperate need of a smile or an encouraging word, and since we don't always know who needs our help, the best strategy is to encourage all those who cross our paths. So today, as you address a classroom, be an enthusiastic booster and a proponent of possibilities. Who knows? Your encouraging words might just change someone's day . . . or someone's life.

No journey is complete that does not lead through some dark valleys. We can properly comfort others only with the comfort we ourselves have been given by God.

Vance Havner

FAILURE

The plans of the diligent certainly lead to profit, but anyone who is reckless only becomes poor.

Proverbs 21:5 Holman CSB

The occasional disappointments and failures of life are inevitable. Such setbacks are simply the price that we must occasionally pay for our willingness to take risks as we follow our dreams. But even when we encounter bitter disappointments, we must never lose faith.

The reassuring words of Hebrews 10:36 remind us that when we persevere, we will eventually receive that which God has promised. What's required is perseverance, not perfection.

When we encounter the inevitable difficulties of life-here-on-earth, God stands ready to protect us. Our responsibility, of course, is to ask Him for protection. When we call upon Him in heartfelt prayer, He will answer—in His own time and according to His own plan—and He will heal us. And, while we are waiting for God's plans to unfold and for His healing touch to restore us, we can be comforted in the knowledge that our Creator can overcome any obstacle, even if we cannot.

BEYOND FEAR

I cried out to the Lord in my suffering, and he heard me. He set me free from all my fears.

Psalm 34:6 NLT

God is willing to protect us. We, in turn, must open ourselves to His protection and His love. This point is illustrated by the familiar story found in the 4th chapter of Mark: When a terrible storm rose quickly on the Sea of Galilee, the disciples were afraid. Although they had witnessed many miracles, the disciples feared for their lives, so they turned to Jesus, and He calmed the waters and the wind.

Sometimes, we, like the disciples, feel threatened by the storms of life. And when we are fearful, we, too, can turn to Christ for comfort and for courage. The next time you find yourself facing a fear-provoking situation, remember that the One who calmed the wind and the waves is also your personal Savior. Then ask yourself which is stronger: your faith or your fear. The answer, friends, should be obvious: Whatever your challenge, God can handle it. Let Him.

Fear is a self-imposed prison that will keep you from becoming what God intends for you to be.

Rick Warren

FORGIVENESS IS A CHOICE

For if you forgive people their wrongdoing, your heavenly Father will forgive you as well. But if you don't forgive people, your Father will not forgive your wrongdoing.

Matthew 6:14-15 Holman CSB

Forgiveness is a choice. We can either choose to forgive those who have injured us, or not. When we obey God by offering forgiveness to His children, we are blessed. But when we allow bitterness and resentment to poison our hearts, we are tortured by our own shortsightedness.

Do you harbor resentment against anyone? If so, you are faced with an important decision: whether or not to forgive the person who has hurt you. God's instructions are clear: He commands you to forgive. God doesn't suggest that you forgive or request that you forgive; He commands it. Period.

To forgive or not to forgive: that is the question. The answer should be obvious. The time to forgive is now because tomorrow may be too late . . . for you.

Forgiveness is not an emotion. Forgiveness is an act of the will, and the will can function regardless of the temperature of the heart.

Corrie ten Boom

BE GENEROUS

Be generous: Invest in acts of charity. Charity yields high returns.

Ecclesiastes 11:1 MSG

God's heart overflows with generosity and mercy. And as believers in a loving God, we must, to the best of our abilities, imitate our Heavenly Father. Because God has been so incredibly generous with us, we, in turn must be generous with others.

Jesus has much to teach us about generosity. He teaches that the most esteemed men and women are not the self-congratulatory leaders of society but are, instead, the humblest of servants (Matthew 23:11-12).

If you were being graded on generosity, how would you score? Would you earn "A"s in philanthropy and humility? Hopefully so. But if your grades could stand a little improvement, today is the perfect day to begin.

Today, you may feel the urge to hoard your blessings. Don't do it. Instead, give generously to your neighbors, and do so without fanfare. Find a need and fill it . . . humbly. Lend a helping hand and share a word of kindness . . . anonymously. This is God's way.

The mind grows by taking in, but the heart grows by giving out.

Warren Wiersbe

GOD'S BLESSINGS

The Lord bless you and protect you; the Lord make His face shine on you, and be gracious to you.

Numbers 6:24-25 Holman CSB

Do you know how richly you have been blessed? Well, God's gifts are actually too numerous to count, but you are wise to inventory as many blessings as you can, as often as you can.

Elisabeth Elliot noted, "It is always possible to be thankful for what is given rather than to complain about what is not given. One or the other becomes a habit of life." And Gloria Gaither observed, "God has promised that if we harvest well with the tools of thanksgiving, there will be seeds for planting in the spring."

Are you taking God's gifts for granted? If so, you are doing a disservice to your Creator and to yourself. And the best way to resolve that problem is make this day (and every day) a time for celebration and praise. Starting now.

We prevent God from giving us the great spiritual gifts He has in store for us, because we do not give thanks for daily gifts.

Dietrich Bonhoeffer

HIS GUIDANCE

When people do not accept divine guidance, they run wild.
But whoever obeys the law is happy.

Proverbs 29:18 NLT

The Bible promises that God will guide you if you let Him. Your job, of course, is to let Him. But sometimes, you will be tempted to do otherwise. Sometimes, you'll be tempted to go along with the crowd; other times, you'll be tempted to do things your way, not God's way. When you feel those temptations, resist them.

What will you allow to guide you through the coming day: your own desires (or, for that matter, the desires of your friends)? Or will you allow God to lead the way? The answer should be obvious. You should let God be your guide. When you do, your next step will be the right one.

If we want to hear God's voice, we must surrender our minds and hearts to Him.

Billy Graham

—TODAY'S PRAYER—

Dear Lord, You always stand ready to guide me. Let me accept your guidance, today and every day of my life. Lead me, Father, and let me trust You completely, so that my life can be a tribute to Your grace, to Your mercy, to Your love, and to Your Son. Amen

THE GOOD NEWS

Then he said, "Go into the world. Go everywhere and announce the Message of God's good news to one and all."

Mark 16:15 MSG

The Good News of Jesus Christ should be shouted from the rooftops by believers the world over. But all too often, it is not. For a variety of reasons, many Christians keep their beliefs to themselves, and when they do, the world suffers because of their failure to speak up.

Paul offered a message to believers of every generation when he wrote, "God has not given us a spirit of timidity" (2 Timothy 1:7 NASB). Paul's meaning is clear: When sharing our testimonies, we must be courageous, forthright, and unashamed. As believers in Christ, we know how He has touched our hearts and changed our lives. Now is the time to share our personal testimonies with others.

The old familiar hymn begins, "What a friend we have in Jesus...." No truer words were ever penned. Jesus is the sovereign friend and ultimate Savior of mankind. Christ showed enduring love for His believers by willingly sacrificing His own life so that we might have eternal life. Let us love Him, praise Him, and share His message of salvation with our neighbors and with the world.

HONESTY

. . . and put on the new self, which in the likeness of God has been created in righteousness and holiness of the truth. Therefore, laying aside falsehood, speak truth, each one of you, with his neighbor, for we are members of one another.

Ephesians 4:24-25 NASB

It has been said on many occasions and in many ways that honesty is the best policy. For believers, it is far more important to note that honesty is God's policy. And if we are to be servants worthy of our Savior, Jesus Christ, we must be honest and forthright in our communications with others.

Sometimes, honesty is difficult; sometimes, honesty is painful; always, honesty is God's commandment. In the Book of Exodus, God did not command, "Thou shalt not bear false witness when it is convenient." And He didn't say, "Thou shalt not bear false witness most of the time." God said, "Thou shalt not bear false witness against thy neighbor." Period.

Sometime soon, perhaps even today, you will be tempted to bend the truth or perhaps even to break it. Resist that temptation. Truth is God's way...and it must also be yours. Period.

The single most important element in any human relationship is honesty—with oneself, with God, and with others.

Catherine Marshall

THE GOOD SAMARITAN

Then a Samaritan traveling down the road came to where the hurt man was. When he saw the man, he felt very sorry for him. The Samaritan went to him, poured olive oil and wine on his wounds, and bandaged them. Then he put the hurt man on his own donkey and took him to an inn where he cared for him.

Luke 10:33-34 NCV

Sometimes we would like to help make the world a better place, but we're not sure of the best way to do it. Jesus told the story of the "Good Samaritan," a man who helped a fellow traveler when no one else would. We, too, should be good Samaritans when we encounter people who need our help.

The words of Jesus are unambiguous: "Freely you have received, freely give" (Matthew 10:8 NIV). As followers of Christ, we are commanded to be generous with our friends, with our families, and with those in need. We must give freely of our time, our possessions, and, most especially, our love.

Today, take God's words to heart and make this pledge: Wherever you happen to be, be a good Samaritan. Somebody near you needs your assistance, and you need the spiritual rewards that will be yours when you lend a helping hand.

HE OVERCOMES

I say to myself, "The Lord is mine, so I hope in him."
Lamentations 3:24 NCV

There are few sadder sights on earth than the sight of a person who has lost all hope. In difficult times, hope can be elusive, but Christians need never lose it. After all, God is good; His love endures; He has promised His children the gift of eternal life.

If you find yourself falling into the spiritual traps of worry and discouragement, consider the words of Jesus. It was Christ who promised, "In the world you will have tribulation; but be of good cheer, I have overcome the world" (John 16:33 NKJV). This world is, indeed, a place of trials and tribulations, but as believers, we are secure. God has promised us peace, joy, and eternal life. And, of course, God always keeps His promises.

Love is the seed of all hope. It is the enticement to trust, to risk, to try, and to go on.

Gloria Gaither

—TODAY'S PRAYER—

Dear Lord, make me a hope-filled Christian. If I become discouraged, let me turn to You. If I grow weary, let me seek strength in You. In every aspect of my life, I will trust You, Father, today and forever. Amen

LAUGHTER IS MEDICINE

A happy heart makes the face cheerful....

Proverbs 15:13 NIV

Laughter is medicine for the soul, but sometimes, amid the stresses of the day, we forget to take our medicine. Instead of viewing our world with a mixture of optimism and humor, we allow worries and distractions to rob us of the joy that God intends for our lives. Today, as you go about your daily activities, approach life with a smile and a chuckle. After all, God created laughter for a reason…and Father indeed knows best. So laugh!

Humor ought to be consecrated and used for the cause of Christ.

C. H. Spurgeon

When you have good, healthy relationships with your family and friends you're more prompted to laugh and not to take yourself so seriously.

Dennis Swanberg

—TODAY'S PRAYER—

Lord, when I begin to take myself or my life too seriously, let me laugh. When I rush from place to place, slow me down, Lord, and let me laugh. Put a smile on my face, Dear Lord, and let me share that smile with all who cross my path . . . and let me laugh. Amen

LOVE NOW

If anyone boasts, "I love God," and goes right on hating his brother or sister, thinking nothing of it, he is a liar. If he won't love the person he can see, how can he love the God he can't see? The command we have from Christ is blunt: Loving God includes loving people. You've got to love both.

1 John 4:20-21 MSG

The familiar words of 1st Corinthians 13 remind us of the importance of love. Faith is important, of course. So too is hope. But love is more important still.

Christ showed His love for us on the cross, and, as Christians, we are called upon to return Christ's love by sharing it. We are commanded (not advised, not encouraged...commanded!) to love one another just as Christ loved us (John 13:34). That's a tall order, but as Christians, we are obligated to follow it.

Sometimes love is easy (puppies and sleeping children come to mind) and sometimes love is hard (fallible human beings come to mind). But God's Word is clear: We are to love all our friends and neighbors, not just the lovable ones. So today, take time to spread Christ's message by word and by example. And the greatest of these is, of course, is example.

The Christian life has two different dimensions: faith toward God and love toward men. You cannot separate the two.

Warren Wiersbe

MODERATION

Moderation is better than muscle, self-control better than political power.

Proverbs 16:32 MSG

Moderation and wisdom are traveling companions. If we are wise, we must learn to temper our appetites, our desires, and our impulses. When we do, we are blessed, in part, because God has created a world in which temperance is rewarded and intemperance is inevitably punished.

Would you like to improve your life? Then harness your appetites and restrain your impulses. Moderation is difficult, of course; it is especially difficult in a prosperous society such as ours. But the rewards of moderation are numerous and long-lasting. Claim those rewards today.

No one can force you to moderate your appetites. The decision to live temperately (and wisely) is yours and yours alone. And so are the consequences.

—TODAY'S PRAYER—

Dear Lord, give me the wisdom to be moderate and self-disciplined. Let me strive to do Your will here on earth, and as I do, let me find contentment and balance. Let me be a disciplined believer, Father, today and every day. Amen

WAIT AND WORK

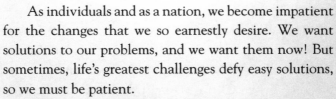

God blesses the people who patiently endure testing. Afterward they will receive the crown of life that God has promised to those who love him.

James 1:12 NLT

As individuals and as a nation, we become impatient for the changes that we so earnestly desire. We want solutions to our problems, and we want them now! But sometimes, life's greatest challenges defy easy solutions, so we must be patient.

Psalm 37:7 commands us to wait patiently for God, but, for most of us, waiting quietly for Him is difficult. Why? Because we are fallible human beings who seek solutions to our problems today, if not sooner. We seek to manage our lives according to our own timetables, not God's. Still, God instructs us to be patient in all things, and that is as it should be. After all, think about how patient God has been with us.

Those who have had to wait and work for happiness seem to enjoy it more, because they never take it for granted.

Barbara Johnson

PRAISE FOR THE SAVIOR

So that at the name of Jesus every knee should bow—of those who are in heaven and on earth and under the earth—and every tongue should confess that Jesus Christ is Lord, to the glory of God the Father.

Philippians 2:10-11 Holman CSB

The words by Fanny Crosby are familiar: "This is my story, this is my song, praising my Savior, all the day long." And, as believers who have been saved by the blood of a risen Christ, we must do exactly as the song instructs: we must praise our Savior many times each day.

Worship and praise must be woven into the fabric of everything we do. Otherwise, we quickly lose perspective as we fall prey to the demands of everyday life.

Do you sincerely seek to be a worthy servant of the One who has given you eternal love and eternal life? Then praise Him for who He is and for what He has done for you. And don't just praise Him on Sunday morning. Praise Him all day long, every day, for as long as you live . . . and then for all eternity.

Praise and thank God for who He is and for what He has done for you.

Billy Graham

RENEWAL

. . . the inward man is being renewed day by day.

2 Corinthians 4:16 NKJV

When we genuinely lift our hearts and prayers to God, He renews our strength. Are you almost too weary to lift your head? Then bow it. Offer your concerns and your fears to your Father in Heaven. He is always at your side, offering His love and His strength.

Are you troubled or anxious? Take your anxieties to God in prayer. Are you weak or worried? Delve deeply into God's Holy Word and sense His presence in the quiet moments of the early morning. Are you spiritually exhausted? Call upon fellow believers to support you, and call upon Christ to renew your spirit and your life. Your Savior will never let you down. To the contrary, He will always lift you up if you ask Him to. So what, dear friend, are you waiting for?

—TODAY'S PRAYER—

Dear Lord, You have the power to make all things new. When I grow weary, let me turn my thoughts and my prayers to You. When I am discouraged, restore my faith in You. Renew my strength, Father, and let me draw comfort and courage from Your promises and from Your unending love. Amen

SEEKING GOD

The Lord is with you when you are with Him. If you seek Him, He will be found by you.

2 Chronicles 15:2 Holman CSB

Where is God? He is everywhere you have ever been and everywhere you will ever go. He is with you night and day; He knows your every thought; He hears your every heartbeat.

Sometimes, in the crush of your daily duties, God may seem far away. Or sometimes, when the disappointments and sorrows of life leave you breathless, God may seem distant, but He is not. When you earnestly seek God, you will find Him because He is here, waiting patiently for you to reach out to Him . . . right here . . . right now.

Pour out your heart to God and tell Him how you feel. Be real, be honest, and when you get it all out, you'll start to feel the gradual covering of God's comforting presence.

Bill Hybels

We rarely discover anything monumental about God without discovering something momentous about ourselves. With every revelation comes an invitation to adjust our lives to what we have seen.

Beth Moore

YOU DESERVE A SMILE

God's servant must not be argumentative, but a gentle listener and a teacher who keeps cool, working firmly but patiently with those who refuse to obey. You never know how or when God might sober them up with a change of heart and a turning to the truth.

2 Timothy 2:24-25 MSG

Because you are a teacher, you deserve a big smile. Henry Adams correctly observed, "A teacher affects eternity; he can never tell where his influence stops." And, those words have never been more true than they are today. We live in a difficult, temptation-filled world—a world in which our young people need the leadership provided by teachers who know and love God.

Whether you teach graduate school or Sunday School, whether you lecture at seminary or at Vacation Bible School, you are God's emissary, a person charged with molding lives—a truly awesome responsibility. God takes your teaching duties very seriously, and so should you.

As a teacher, you're helping the Creator reshape eternity. It's a big job, but don't worry; you and God can handle it.

Let us look upon our children; let us love them and train them as children of the covenant and children of the promise. These are the children of God.

Andrew Murray

ADVERSITY

Whatever has been born of God conquers the world. This is the victory that has conquered the world: our faith.

1 John 5:4 Holman CSB

Teachers of every generation have experienced challenges, and this generation is no different. But, today's teachers face difficulties that previous generations could have scarcely imagined. Thankfully, although the world continues to change, God's love remains constant. And, He remains ready to comfort us and strengthen us whenever we turn to Him.

Where is the best place to take our worries? We should take them to God. We should take our troubles to Him, and our fears, our dilemmas and our sorrows. We should seek protection from the One who cannot be moved. Then, when we have genuinely turned our concerns over to God, we should worry less and trust Him more, because God is trustworthy…and we are protected.

In order to realize the worth of the anchor, we need to feel the stress of the storm.

Corrie ten Boom

LOOK UPWARD

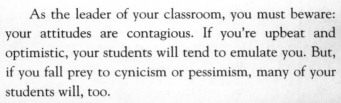

Set your minds on what is above, not on what is on the earth.

Colossians 3:2 Holman CSB

As the leader of your classroom, you must beware: your attitudes are contagious. If you're upbeat and optimistic, your students will tend to emulate you. But, if you fall prey to cynicism or pessimism, many of your students will, too.

How will you direct your thoughts today? Will you obey the words of Philippians 4:8 by dwelling upon those things that are honorable, true, and worthy of praise? Or will you allow your thoughts to be hijacked by the negativity that seems to dominate our troubled world?

God intends that you experience joy and abundance, but He will not force His joy upon you; you must claim it for yourself. So, today and every day hereafter, focus your thoughts and your energies upon "whatever is commendable." Celebrate life, and before you know it, you'll find many of your students are joining in the celebration.

No matter how little we can change about our circumstances, we always have a choice about our attitude toward the situation.

Vonette Bright

THIS IS THE DAY

This is the day the Lord has made; let us rejoice and be glad in it.

Psalm 118:24 Holman CSB

The 118th Psalm reminds us that today, like every other day, is a cause for celebration. God gives us this day; He fills it to the brim with possibilities, and He challenges us to use it for His purposes. Today is a non-renewable resource—once it's gone, it's gone forever. Our responsibility—as Christians and as teachers— is to use this day in the service of God's will as we share His wisdom and His love.

Do not so contemplate eternity that you waste today.

Vance Havner

The one word in the spiritual vocabulary is now.

Oswald Chambers

—TODAY'S PRAYER—

Dear Lord, You have given me so many reasons to celebrate. Today, let me choose an attitude of cheerfulness. Let me be a joyful Christian, Lord, quick to laugh and slow to anger. And, let me share Your goodness with my family, my friends, my neighbors, and my students, this day and every day. Amen

CHRIST'S LOVE

Just as the Father has loved Me, I also have loved you. Remain in My love.

John 15:9 Holman CSB

Christ's love for you is personal. His love for you is intimate. He loves you so much that He gave His life in order that you might spend all eternity with Him. Christ loves you individually and faithfully; His is a love unbounded by time or circumstance.

Christ's love is the cornerstone of the Christian faith—is it the cornerstone of your life? Are you willing to experience an intimate relationship with Jesus, or are you determined to keep Him at a "safe" distance? Your Savior is waiting patiently; don't make Him wait a single minute longer. Embrace His love today.

Jesus is all compassion. He never betrays us.

Catherine Marshall

—TODAY'S PRAYER—

Dear Jesus, I am humbled by Your love and mercy. You went to Calvary so that I might have eternal life. Thank You, Jesus, for Your priceless gift, and for Your love. You loved me first, Lord, and I will return Your love today and forever. Amen

A CLEAR CONSCIENCE

Now the goal of our instruction is love from a pure heart, a good conscience, and a sincere faith.

1 Timothy 1:5 Holman CSB

Simply put, a guilty conscience has the power to torment us. And thankfully, the opposite is also true: Few things in life provide more contentment than a clear conscience—a clear conscience that results from the knowledge that we are obeying God's commandments.

Thoughtful teachers (like you) understand the importance of wise choices and the rewards of a clear conscience . . . and thoughtful teachers (like you) share that message with their students.

Your conscience is your alarm system. It's your protection.

Charles Stanley

—TODAY'S PRAYER—

Dear Lord, You speak to me through the Bible, through teachers, and through friends. And, Father, You speak to me through that still, small voice that warns me when I stray from Your will. In these quiet moments and throughout the day, show me Your plan for my life, Lord, that I might serve You. Amen

DIFFICULT DAYS

Should we accept only good from God and not adversity?
Job 2:10 Holman CSB

All of us face those occasional days when the traffic jams and the dog gobbles up the homework. But, when we find ourselves overtaken by the minor frustrations of life, we must catch ourselves, take a deep breath, and lift our thoughts upward.

Although we are here on earth struggling to rise above the distractions of the day, we need never struggle alone. God is here—eternally and faithfully, with infinite patience and love—and, if we reach out to Him, He will restore perspective and peace to our souls.

When life is difficult, God wants us to have a faith that trusts and waits.

Kay Arthur

—TODAY'S PRAYER—

Lord, on difficult days, I will turn to You for my strength. In times of sadness, I will put my trust in You. In times of frustration, I will find peace in You. And every day, whether I am happy or sad, I will praise You for Your glorious works and for the gift of Your Son. Amen

DREAMS

When dreams come true, there is life and joy.

Proverbs 13:12 NLT

Are you willing to dream big dreams? Hopefully so; after all, God promises that we can do "all things" through Him. Yet most of us, even the most devout among us, live far below our potential. We take half measures; we dream small dreams; we waste precious time and energy on the distractions of the world. But God has other plans for us. Our Creator intends that we live faithfully, hopefully, courageously, and abundantly. He knows that we are capable of so much more; and He wants us to do the things we're capable of doing; and He wants us to start doing those things now.

Set goals so big that unless God helps you, you will be a miserable failure.

Bill Bright

—TODAY'S PRAYER—

Dear Lord, give me the courage to dream and the faithfulness to trust in Your perfect plan. When I am worried or weary, give me strength for today and hope for tomorrow. Keep me mindful of Your healing power, Your infinite love, and Your eternal salvation. Amen

ETERNAL LIFE

For God loved the world in this way: He gave His only Son, so that everyone who believes in Him will not perish but have eternal life.

John 3:16 Holman CSB

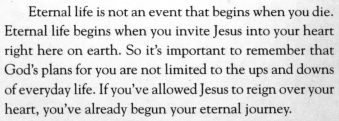

Eternal life is not an event that begins when you die. Eternal life begins when you invite Jesus into your heart right here on earth. So it's important to remember that God's plans for you are not limited to the ups and downs of everyday life. If you've allowed Jesus to reign over your heart, you've already begun your eternal journey.

As mere mortals, our vision for the future, like our lives here on earth, is limited. God's vision is not burdened by such limitations: His plans extend throughout all eternity.

Let us praise the Creator for His priceless gift, and let us share the Good News with all who cross our paths. We return our Father's love by accepting His grace and by sharing His message and His love. When we do, we are blessed here on earth and throughout all eternity.

Teach us to set our hopes on heaven, to hold firmly to the promise of eternal life, so that we can withstand the struggles and storms of this world.

Max Lucado

FAITHFULNESS

A faithful man will have many blessings.

Proverbs 28:20 Holman CSB

Every life—including yours—is a series of successes and failures, celebrations and disappointments, joys and sorrows. Every step of the way, through every triumph and tragedy, God will stand by your side and strengthen you . . . if you have faith in Him. Jesus taught His disciples that if they had faith, they could move mountains. You can too.

When a suffering woman sought healing by merely touching the hem of His cloak, Jesus replied, "Daughter, be of good comfort; thy faith hath made thee whole" (Matthew 9:22 KJV). The message to believers of every generation is clear: we must live by faith today and every day.

When you place your faith, your trust, indeed your life in the hands of Christ Jesus, you'll be amazed at the marvelous things He can do with you and through you. So strengthen your faith through praise, through worship, through Bible study, and through prayer. And trust God's plans. With Him, all things are possible, and He stands ready to open a world of possibilities to you . . . if you have faith.

WALK AS HE WALKED

But whoever keeps His word, truly in him the love of God is perfected. This is how we know we are in Him: the one who says he remains in Him should walk just as He walked.

1 John 2:5-6 Holman CSB

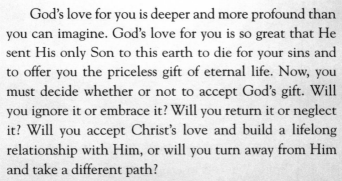

God's love for you is deeper and more profound than you can imagine. God's love for you is so great that He sent His only Son to this earth to die for your sins and to offer you the priceless gift of eternal life. Now, you must decide whether or not to accept God's gift. Will you ignore it or embrace it? Will you return it or neglect it? Will you accept Christ's love and build a lifelong relationship with Him, or will you turn away from Him and take a different path?

Your decision to allow Christ to reign over your heart is the pivotal decision of your life. It is a decision that you cannot ignore. It is a decision that is yours and yours alone. Accept God's gift now: allow His Son to preside over your heart, your thoughts, and your life, starting this very instant.

When we truly walk with God throughout our day, life slowly starts to fall into place.

Bill Hybels

FULFILLMENT

For You, O God, have tested us; You have refined us as silver is refined. You brought us into the net; You laid affliction on our backs. You have caused men to ride over our heads; we went through fire and through water; but You brought us out to rich fulfillment.

Psalm 66:10–12 NKJV

Everywhere we turn, or so it seems, the world promises fulfillment, contentment, and happiness. But the contentment the world offers is fleeting and incomplete. Thankfully the fulfillment God offers is all encompassing and everlasting.

Sometimes, amid the inevitable hustle and bustle of daily living, we can lose sight of the real joys of life as we wrestle with the challenges that confront us. Yet fulfillment is available to people who seek it in proper places and in proper ways.

The thoughts you think, the actions you take, the prayers you pray, and the people you serve all have a powerful influence on the fulfillment that you experience.

Aristotle observed, "Happiness depends upon ourselves." And his words still apply. If you want to find fulfillment, you'll have to find it for yourself . . . starting now and ending never.

FOCUSING ON HIS LOVE

*For God loved the world in this way: He gave His only Son,
so that everyone who believes in Him will not perish but have
eternal life.*

John 3:16 Holman CSB

Make no mistake about it: God loves our world. He loves it so much, in fact, that He sent His only begotten Son to die for our sins. And now we, as believers, are challenged to return God's love by obeying His commandments and honoring His Son.

When you open your heart and accept God's love, you are transformed not just for today, but for all eternity. When you accept the Father's love, you feel differently about yourself, your world, your neighbors, your family, and your church. When you experience God's presence and invite His Son into your heart, you feel the need to share His message and to obey His commandments.

God loved this world so much that He sent His Son to save it. And now only one real question remains for you: what will you do in response to God's love? The answer should be obvious: If you haven't already done so, accept Jesus Christ as your Savior. He's waiting patiently for you, but please don't make Him wait another minute longer.

A ROYAL LAW

If you really carry out the royal law prescribed in Scripture,
You shall love your neighbor as yourself, you are doing well.
James 2:8 Holman CSB

As Christians, we are instructed to be courteous and compassionate. As believers, we are called to be gracious, humble, gentle, and kind. But sometimes, we fall short. Sometimes, amid the busyness and confusion of everyday life, we may neglect to share a kind word or a kind deed. This oversight hurts others, and it hurts us as well.

Today, slow yourself down and be alert for those who need your smile, your kind words, or your helping hand. Make kindness a centerpiece of your dealings with others. They will be blessed, and you will be, too. So make this promise to yourself and keep it: honor Christ by obeying His Golden Rule.

—TODAY'S PRAYER—

Dear Lord, let me treat others as I wish to be treated. Because I expect kindness, let me be kind. Because I wish to be loved, let me be loving. Because I need forgiveness, let me be merciful. In all things, Lord, let me live by the Golden Rule that is the commandment of Your Son Jesus. Amen

CLAIM THE JOY

So I recommend having fun, because there is nothing better for people to do in this world than to eat, drink, and enjoy life. That way they will experience some happiness along with all the hard work God gives them.

Ecclesiastes 8:15 NLT

Happiness depends less upon our circumstances than upon our thoughts. When we turn our thoughts to God, to His gifts, and to His glorious creation, we experience the joy that God intends for His children. But, when we focus on the negative aspects of life, we suffer needlessly.

Do you sincerely want to be a happy Christian? Then set your mind and your heart upon God's love and His grace. The fullness of life in Christ is available to all who seek it and claim it. Count yourself among that number. Seek first the salvation that is available through a personal relationship with Jesus Christ, and then claim the joy, the peace, and the spiritual abundance that the Shepherd offers His sheep.

No man should desire to be happy who is not at the same time holy. He should spend his efforts in seeking to know and do the will of God, leaving to Christ the matter of how happy he shall be.

A. W. Tozer

GOD'S POLICY

The godly are directed by their honesty.

Proverbs 11:5 NLT

From the time we are children, we are taught that honesty is the best policy. And, in the classroom, we instruct our students that honesty is also the school's policy. But, honesty is not just the best policy or the school's policy, it is also God's policy. If we are to be servants worthy of His holy blessings, we must remember that truth is not just the best way, it is God's way. May we teach truth and practice it . . . but not necessarily in that order.

We can teach our children that being honest protects from guilt and provides for a clear conscience.

Josh McDowell

—TODAY'S PRAYER—

Dear Lord, let me walk in truth and let me share Your truth. As a teacher, I am a role model to my students. Make me Your worthy servant so that others might see my love for You reflected in my words and my deeds. Amen

SPIRITUAL MATURITY

But grow in the grace and knowledge of our Lord and Savior Jesus Christ.

2 Peter 3:18 NIV

The journey toward spiritual maturity lasts a lifetime. As Christians, we can and should continue to grow in the love and the knowledge of our Savior as long as we live.

When we cease to grow, either emotionally or spiritually, we do ourselves a profound disservice. But, if we study God's Word, if we obey His commandments, and if we live in the center of His will, we will not be "stagnant" believers; we will, instead, be growing Christians . . . and that's exactly what God intends for us to be.

Life is a series of choices and decisions. Each day, we make countless decisions that can bring us closer to God . . . or not. When we live according to the principles contained in God's Holy Word, we embark upon a journey of spiritual maturity that results in life abundant and life eternal.

No matter what we are going through, no matter how long the waiting for answers, of one thing we may be sure. God is faithful. He keeps His promises. What He starts, He finishes . . . including His perfect work in us.

Gloria Gaither

A BEAUTIFUL LANDSCAPE

Make me hear joy and gladness.

Psalm 51:8 NKJV

As you look at the landscape of your life, do you see opportunities, possibilities, and blessings, or do you focus, instead, upon the more negative scenery? Do you spend more time counting your blessings or your misfortunes? If you've acquired the unfortunate habit of focusing too intently upon the negative aspects of life, then your spiritual vision is in need of correction.

Today is yet another gift from God, and it presents yet another opportunity to thank Him for His gifts . . . or not. And if you're wise, you'll give thanks early and often.

The way that you choose to view the scenery around you will have a profound impact on the quality, the tone, and the direction of your life. The more you focus on the beauty that surrounds you, the more beautiful your own life becomes.

—TODAY'S PRAYER—

Thank You, Lord, for Your infinite love. Make me an optimistic Christian, Father, as I place my hope and my trust in You. Amen

PERSEVERANCE

I have fought the good fight, I have finished the race, I have kept the faith.

2 Timothy 4:7 Holman CSB

In a world filled with roadblocks and stumbling blocks, we need strength, courage, and perseverance. And, as an example of perfect perseverance, we need look no further than our Savior, Jesus Christ.

Jesus finished what He began. Despite the torture He endured, despite the shame of the cross, Jesus was steadfast in His faithfulness to God. We, too, must remain faithful, especially during times of hardship.

Perhaps you are in a hurry for God to reveal His plans for your life. If so, be forewarned: God operates on His own timetable, not yours. Sometimes, God may answer your prayers with silence, and when He does, you must patiently persevere. In times of trouble, you must remain steadfast and trust in the merciful goodness of your Heavenly Father. Whatever your problem, He can handle it. Your job is to keep persevering until He does.

Failure is one of life's most powerful teachers. How we handle our failures determines whether we're going to simply "get by" in life or "press on."

Beth Moore

SUCCESS ACCORDING TO GOD

Trust in the Lord and do good. Then you will live safely in the land and prosper.

Psalm 37:3 NLT

Do you want to be successful? Then here are a few things you should do: 1. Put God first . . . in every aspect of your life, including your career. 2. Wherever you happen to be, be the best you can be: Giving your best is habit-forming, so give your best every time you go to work. 3. Keep learning: The future belongs to those who are willing to do the work that's required to prepare for it. 4. Have patience and perseverance . . . Rome wasn't built in a day, and the same goes for your life. 5. When you make a wrong turn and find yourself at the end of a dead-end street . . . turn around sooner rather than later.

And above all, remember this: genuine success has little to do with fame or fortune; it has everything to do with God's gift of love and His promise of salvation.

If you have accepted Christ as your personal Savior, you are already a towering success in the eyes of God, but there is still more that you can do. Your task—as a believer who has been touched by the Creator's grace—is to accept the spiritual abundance and peace that He offers through the person of His Son. Then, you can share the healing message of God's love and His abundance with a world that desperately needs both. When you do, you will have reached the pinnacle of success.

RISK

I can do everything through him that gives me strength.

Philippians 4:13 NIV

As we consider the uncertainties of the future, we are confronted with a powerful temptation: the temptation to "play it safe." Unwilling to move mountains, we fret over molehills. Unwilling to entertain great hopes for the tomorrow, we focus on the unfairness of today. Unwilling to trust God completely, we take timid half-steps when God intends that we make giant leaps.

Today, ask God for the courage to step beyond the boundaries of your doubts. Ask Him to guide you to a place where you can realize your full potential—a place where you are freed from the fear of failure. Ask Him to do His part, and promise Him that you will do your part. Don't ask Him to lead you to a "safe" place; ask Him to lead you to the "right" place . . . and remember: those two places are seldom the same.

When I am secure in Christ, I can afford to take a risk in my life. Only the insecure cannot afford to risk failure. The secure can be honest about themselves; they can admit failure; they are able to seek help and try again. They can change.

John Maxwell

SIN

Let us throw off everything that hinders and the sin that so easily entangles, and let us run with perseverance the race marked out for us.

Hebrews 12:1 NIV

As creatures of free will, we may disobey God whenever we choose, but when we do so, we put ourselves and our loved ones in peril. Why? Because disobedience invites disaster. We cannot sin against God without consequence. We cannot live outside His will without injury. We cannot distance ourselves from God without hardening our hearts. We cannot yield to the ever-tempting distractions of our world and, at the same time, enjoy God's peace.

Sometimes, in a futile attempt to justify our behaviors, we make a distinction between "big" sins and "little" ones. To do so is a mistake of "big" proportions. Sins of all shapes and sizes have the power to do us great harm. And in a world where sin is big business, that's certainly a sobering thought.

A Christian is not sinless, but he does sin less—and less—and less!

Warren Wiersbe

STILLNESS BEFORE GOD

Be still before the Lord and wait patiently for Him.

Psalm 37:7 NIV

We live in a noisy world, a world filled with distractions, frustrations, obligations, and complications. But we must not allow our clamorous world to separate us from God's peace. Instead, we must "be still" so that we might sense the presence of God.

If we are to maintain righteous minds and compassionate hearts, we must take time each day for prayer and for meditation. We must make ourselves still in the presence of our Creator. We must quiet our minds and our hearts so that we might sense God's love, God's will, and God's Son.

Has the busy pace of life robbed you of the peace that might otherwise be yours through Jesus Christ? If so, it's time to reorder your priorities. Nothing is more important than the time you spend with your Savior. So be still and claim the inner peace that is your spiritual birthright: the peace of Jesus Christ. It is offered freely; it has been paid for in full; it is yours for the asking. So ask. And then share.

Be quiet enough to hear God's whisper.

Anonymous

YOUR THOUGHTS

Set your minds on what is above, not on what is on the earth.

Colossians 3:2 Holman CSB

What is your focus today? Are you willing to focus your thoughts on the countless blessings that God has bestowed upon you? Before you answer that question, consider this: the direction of your thoughts will determine, to a surprising extent, the direction of your day and your life.

This day—and every day hereafter—is a chance to celebrate the life that God has given you. It's a chance to celebrate your relationships, your talents, and your opportunities. So focus your thoughts upon the gift of life—and upon the blessings that surround you.

You're a beautiful creation of God, a being of infinite importance. Give thanks for your gifts and share them. Never have the needs—or the opportunities for service—been greater.

No more imperfect thoughts. No more sad memories. No more ignorance. My redeemed body will have a redeemed mind. Grant me a foretaste of that perfect mind as you mirror your thoughts in me today.

Joni Eareckson Tada

WISDOM

Every morning he wakes me. He teaches me to listen like a student. The Lord God helps me learn...

Isaiah 50:4-5 NCV

Wisdom is not accumulated overnight. It is like a savings account that accrues slowly over time, and the person who consistently adds to his account will eventually accumulate a great sum. The secret to success is consistency. Do you seek wisdom for yourself and for your students? Then keep learning and keep motivating them to do likewise. The ultimate source of wisdom, of course, is—first and foremost—the Word of God. When you begin a daily study of God's Word and live according to His commandments, you will become wise...and so, in time, will your students.

The first thing we have to do to receive God's guidance is to reevaluate our current guidance systems.

Bill Hybels

—TODAY'S PRAYER—

Lord, help me to be a teacher who values both education and wisdom. Let me instruct my students by the words that I speak and by the life that I live. My students deserve no less and neither, Dear Lord, do You. Amen

JOY

Make a joyful shout to the Lord, all you lands! Serve the Lord with gladness; Come before His presence with singing.

Psalm 100:1-2 NKJV

Psalm 100 reminds us that, as believers, we have every reason to celebrate: "Shout for joy to the LORD, all the earth. Worship the LORD with gladness" (v. 1-2 NIV). Yet sometimes, amid the inevitable hustle and bustle of life here on earth, we can forfeit—albeit temporarily—the joy that God intends for our lives.

C. H. Spurgeon, the renowned 19th century English clergymen, advised, "Rejoicing is clearly a spiritual command. To ignore it, I need to remind you, is disobedience." As Christians, we are called by our Creator to live abundantly, prayerfully, and joyfully. To do otherwise is to squander His spiritual gifts.

If, today, your heart is heavy, open the door of your soul to the Father and to His only begotten Son. Christ offers you His peace and His joy. Accept it and share it freely, just as Christ has freely shared His joy with you.

You have to look for the joy. Look for the light of God that is hitting your life, and you will find sparkles you didn't know were there.

Barbara Johnson

GOD'S PRESENCE

Be strong and courageous. Do not be terrified; do not be discouraged, for the LORD your God will be with you wherever you go.

Joshua 1:9 NIV

Do you ever wonder if God is really here? If so, you're not the first person to think such thoughts. In fact, some of the biggest heroes in the Bible had their doubts—and so, perhaps, will you. But when questions arise and doubts begin to creep into your mind, remember this: God hasn't gone on vacation; He hasn't left town; and He doesn't have an unlisted number. You can talk with Him any time you feel like it. In fact, He's right here, right now, listening to your thoughts and prayers, watching over your every move.

Sometimes, you will allow yourself to become very busy, and that's when you may be tempted to ignore God. But, when you quiet yourself long enough to acknowledge His presence, God will touch your heart and restore your spirits. By the way, He's ready to talk right now. Are you?

God wants to be in our leisure time as much as He is in our churches and in our work.

Beth Moore

ACCEPTING CHRIST

Yet we know that no one is justified by the works of the law but by faith in Jesus Christ. And we have believed in Christ Jesus, so that we might be justified by faith in Christ and not by the works of the law, because by the works of the law no human being will be justified.

Galatians 2:16 Holman CSB

God's love for you is so great that He sent His only Son to this earth to die for your sins and offer you the priceless gift of eternal life. You must decide whether or not to accept God's gift. The decision, of course, is yours and yours alone, and it has eternal consequences. If you have not already done so, accept God's gift: Accept Christ.

Turn your life over to Christ today, and your life will never be the same.

Billy Graham

Every person who has ever been born has the sovereign right to make this same choice—to receive Jesus Christ by faith as God's revelation of Himself, or to reject Him.

Anne Graham Lotz

FRUSTRATIONS

See to it that no one repays evil for evil to anyone, but always pursue what is good for one another and for all.

1 Thessalonians 5:15 Holman CSB

Teaching, like every job, has its fair share of frustrations—some great, and some small. Sometimes, those frustrations may cause you to reach the boiling point. But here's a word of warning: When you're tempted to lose your temper over the minor inconveniences of the teaching profession, don't give voice to your angry thoughts.

When you make haste to speak angry words, you will inevitably say things that you'll soon regret. Remember: God will help you control your temper if you ask Him to do so. And the time to ask Him is before your temper gets the best of you—not after.

—TODAY'S PRAYER—

Lord, as a frail human being, I can be quick to anger and slow to forgive. But I know, Lord, that Your seek that I live in peace. When I fall prey to pettiness, restore my sense of perspective. When I fall prey to irrational anger, give me inner calm. When I am slow to forgive, Lord, keep me mindful of Your commandment that I love my neighbor as myself. Let me follow in the footsteps of Your Son Jesus who forgave His persecutors, and as I turn away from anger, let me claim for myself the peace that You intend for my life. Amen

READ HIS BOOK

There's nothing like the written Word of God for showing you the way to salvation through faith in Christ Jesus. Every part of Scripture is God-breathed and useful one way or another, showing us truth, exposing our rebellion, correcting our mistakes, training us to live God's way. Through the Word we are put together and shaped up for the tasks God has for us.

2 Timothy 3:15-17 MSG

If you really want to know God, you should read the book He wrote. It's called the Bible, and it is one of the most important tools that God uses to direct your steps and transform your life.

As you seek to build a deeper relationship with your Creator, you must decide whether God's Word will be bright spotlight that guides your path every day or a tiny night light that occasionally flickers in the dark. The decision to study the Bible—or not—is yours and yours alone. But make no mistake: the way that you choose to use your Bible will have a profound impact on you and your loved ones. Your Bible is waiting patiently on your bookshelf . . . now, what are you going to do about it?

You all have by you a large treasure of divine knowledge, in that you have the Bible in your hands; therefore be not contented in possessing but little of this treasure.

Jonathan Edwards

CHILDREN

I have no greater joy than this: to hear that my children are walking in the truth.

3 John 1:4 Holman CSB

Every child is different, but every child is similar in this respect: he or she is a priceless gift from the Father above. And, with the Father's gift comes immense responsibilities for parents and teachers alike. Even on those difficult days when the classroom is in an uproar and the papers are piled to the ceiling, wise teachers never forget the overriding goal of their profession: shaping young minds. The very best teachers shape those minds with love, with discipline, and with God.

Our children are our most precious resource. May we, as responsible Christians and dedicated teachers, pray for children here at home and for children around the world. Every child is God's child. May we, as concerned adults, behave—and pray—accordingly.

—TODAY'S PRAYER—

Today, Dear Lord, I pray for all Your children. This world holds countless dangers and temptations. I pray that our children may be protected from harm, and that they may discover Your will, Your love, and Your Son. Amen

COMMITMENT

If you do not stand firm in your faith, then you will not stand at all.

Isaiah 7:9 Holman CSB

Do you value your relationship with God . . . and do you tell Him so many times each day? Hopefully so. But if you find yourself overwhelmed by the demands of everyday life, you may find yourself scurrying from place to place with scarcely a spare moment to think about your relationship with the Creator. If so, you're simply too busy for your own good.

God calls upon you to worship Him, to obey His commandments, and to accept His Son as your Savior. When you do, God will bless you in ways that you can scarcely imagine. So why not let Him bless you today, tomorrow, and every day of your life?

—TODAY'S PRAYER—

Dear Lord, make me a person of unwavering commitment to You and to my family. Guide me away from the temptations and distractions of this world, so that I might honor You with my thoughts, my actions, and my prayers. Amen

COURTESY

Be hospitable to one another without grumbling.

1 Peter 4:9 NKJV

Does the Bible instruct us in matters of etiquette and courtesy? Of course it does. The words of Matthew 7:12 are clear: "In everything, therefore, treat people the same way you want them to treat you, for this is the Law and the Prophets" (NASB).

The Bible doesn't instruct, "In some things, treat people as you wish to be treated." And, it doesn't say, "From time to time, treat others with kindness." The Bible instructs us to treat others as we wish to be treated in every aspect of our daily lives.

Today, try to be a little kinder than necessary to family members, friends, and total strangers. And as you consider all the things God has done for you, honor Him with your kind words and good deeds. He deserves no less, and neither do your loved ones.

When you extend hospitality to others, you're not trying to impress people; you're trying to reflect God to them.

Max Lucado

DISCIPLINE

For God has not called us to impurity, but to sanctification.
1 Thessalonians 4:7 Holman CSB

God doesn't reward laziness, misbehavior, or apathy. To the contrary, He expects believers to behave with dignity and discipline. God's Word reminds us again and again that our Creator expects us to lead disciplined lives—and we must take God at His Word, despite temptations to do otherwise.

We live in a world in which leisure is glorified and indifference is often glamorized. But God has other plans. He did not create us for lives of mediocrity; He created us for far greater things.

Life's greatest rewards seldom fall into our laps; to the contrary, our greatest accomplishments usually require lots of work, which is perfectly fine with God. After all, He knows that we're up to the task, and He has big plans for us; may we, as disciplined believers, always be worthy of those plans.

—TODAY'S PRAYER—

Lord, I want to be a disciplined believer. Let me use my time wisely, and let me teach others by the faithfulness of my conduct, today and every day. Amen

PROMOTING GOOD WORKS

And let us be concerned about one another in order to promote love and good works.

Hebrews 10:24 Holman CSB

Life is a team sport, and all of us need occasional pats on the back from our teammates. As Christians, we are called upon to spread the Good News of Christ, and we are also called to spread a message of encouragement and hope to the world.

Whether you realize it or not, many people with whom you come in contact every day are in desperate need of a smile or an encouraging word. The world can be a difficult place, and countless friends and family members may be troubled by the challenges of everyday life. Since you don't always know who needs our help, the best strategy is to try to encourage all the people who cross your path. So today, be a world-class source of encouragement to everyone you meet. Never has the need been greater.

We urgently need people who encourage and inspire us to move toward God and away from the world's enticing pleasures.

Jim Cymbala

LIVING BY FAITH

Now the just shall live by faith.

Hebrews 10:38 NKJV

Life is a grand adventure made great by faith. Enduring faith is first experienced at a mother's knee. There, the child learns to trust not only in the parent but also the world.

Helen Keller observed, "Faith is a spiritual spotlight that illuminates the path."

And Helen Hayes noted, "I have doubted; I have wandered off the path; I have been lost. But, I have always returned; my faith has wavered but has saved me."

So if you're looking for a message to share with future generations, preach the gospel of faith: faith in the future, faith in one's fellow man, and faith in the Hand that shapes eternity. No message is more important.

—TODAY'S PRAYER—

Father, in the dark moments of my life, help me to remember that You are always near and that You can overcome any challenge. Keep me mindful of Your love and Your power, so that I may live courageously and faithfully today and every day. Amen

YOUR FINANCIAL ROADMAP

Honor the Lord with your wealth and the firstfruits from all your crops. Then your barns will be full, and your wine barrels will overflow with new wine.

Proverbs 3:9-10 NCV

God's Word is not only a roadmap to eternal life, it is also an indispensable guidebook for life here on earth. As such, the Bible has much to say about your life and your finances.

God's Word can be a roadmap to a place of righteous and abundance. Make it your roadmap. God's wisdom can be a light to guide your steps. Claim it as your light. God's Word can be an invaluable tool for crafting a better day and a better life. Make it your tool. And finally, God's Word can help you organize your financial life in such a way that you have less need to worry and more time to celebrate His glorious creation. If that sounds appealing, open your Bible, read its instructions, and follow them.

A Christian seeking God's will must be certain that he has first relinquished control of his life, including his finances, and is truly seeking God's direction.

Larry Burkett

FORGIVENESS NOW

Smart people know how to hold their tongue; their grandeur is to forgive and forget.

Proverbs 19:11 MSG

Do you invest more time than you should reliving the past? Are you troubled by feelings of anger, envy, bitterness, or regret? Do you harbor ill will against someone whom you simply can't seem to forgive? If so, it's time to finally get serious about forgiveness.

Most of us don't spend too much time thinking about forgiveness; we worry, instead, about the injustices we have suffered and the people who inflicted them. God has a better plan: He wants us to live in the present, not the past, and He knows that in order to do so, we must forgive those who have harmed us.

Have you made forgiveness a high priority? Have you sincerely asked God to forgive you for your inability to forgive others? Have you genuinely prayed that bitterness might be swept from your heart? If so, congratulations. If not, perhaps it's time to rearrange your priorities.

In God's curriculum, forgiveness isn't optional; it's a required course.

Criswell Freeman

YOUR HELPING HAND

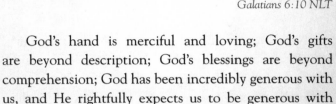

Whenever we have the opportunity, we should do good to everyone, especially to our Christian brothers and sisters.

Galatians 6:10 NLT

God's hand is merciful and loving; God's gifts are beyond description; God's blessings are beyond comprehension; God has been incredibly generous with us, and He rightfully expects us to be generous with others.

The thread of generosity is woven into the very fabric of Christ's teachings. As He sent His disciples out to heal the sick and to spread God's message of salvation, Jesus offered this guiding principle: "Freely you have received, freely give" (Matthew 10:8 NKJV). The principle still applies.

If we are to be disciples of Christ, we must give freely of our time, our possessions, and our love—just as God has been generous with us. As believers, we are blessed here on earth, and we are blessed eternally through God's grace. We can never fully repay God for His gifts, but we can share them with others. And we should.

When somebody needs a helping hand, he doesn't need it tomorrow or the next day. He needs it now, and that's exactly when you should offer to help. Good deeds, if they are really good, happen sooner rather than later.

Marie T. Freeman

A RIGHTEOUS LIFE

This is how we are sure that we have come to know Him: by keeping His commands.

1 John 2:3 Holman CSB

A righteous life has many components: faith, honesty, generosity, discipline, love, kindness, humility, gratitude, and worship, to name but a few. If we seek to follow the steps of Jesus, we must seek to live according to His commandments. In short, we must, to the best of our abilities, live according to the principles contained in God's Holy Word. And then, through our words and our deeds, we must teach our students to do the same.

Let us remember therefore this lesson: That to worship our God sincerely we must evermore begin by hearkening to His voice, and by giving ear to what He commands us. For if every man goes after his own way, we shall wander. We may well run, but we shall never be a whit nearer to the right way, but rather farther away from it.

John Calvin

—TODAY'S PRAYER—

Lord, Your commandments are a perfect guide for my life; let me obey them, and let me lead others to do the same. Give me the wisdom to walk righteously in Your way, Dear Lord, trusting always in You. Amen

GOD'S SOVEREIGNTY

However, each one must live his life in the situation the Lord assigned when God called him.

1 Corinthians 7:17 Holman CSB

God is sovereign. He reigns over the entire universe and He reigns over your little corner of that universe. Your challenge is to recognize God's sovereignty and live in accordance with His commandments. Sometimes, of course, this is easier said than done.

Your Heavenly Father may not always reveal Himself as quickly (or as clearly) as you would like. But rest assured: God is in control, God is here, and God intends to use you in wonderful, unexpected ways. He desires to lead you along a path of His choosing. Your challenge is to watch, to listen, to learn . . . and to follow.

Nothing happens by happenstance. I am not in the hands of fate, nor am I the victim of man's whims or the devil's ploys. There is One who sits above man, above Satan, and above all heavenly hosts as the ultimate authority of all the universe. That One is my God and my Father!

Kay Arthur

LEADERSHIP

Love and truth form a good leader; sound leadership is founded on loving integrity.

Proverbs 20:28 MSG

As a teacher, you are automatically placed in a position of leadership. Unless, you assume firm control over your students, effective learning will not take place in your classroom.

John Maxwell writes, "Great leaders understand that the right attitude will set the right atmosphere, which enables the right response from others." As the leader of your class, it's up to you to set the proper balance between discipline and amusement, between entertainment and scholarship.

Savvy teachers learn to strike an appropriate balance between discipline (which is necessary for maintaining order) and fun (which is necessary for maintaining interest). The rest, of course, is up to the students.

—TODAY'S PRAYER—

Dear Lord, let me be a leader in my classroom and a worthy example to my students. Give me wisdom, courage, compassion, and faith. Let me turn to You, Father, for guidance and for strength in all that I say and do. Amen

LOVING GOD

This is how we know that we love God's children when we love God and obey His commands.

1 John 5:2 Holman CSB

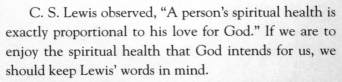

C. S. Lewis observed, "A person's spiritual health is exactly proportional to his love for God." If we are to enjoy the spiritual health that God intends for us, we should keep Lewis' words in mind.

Corrie ten Boom noted, "A bird does not know it can fly before it uses its wings. We learn God's love in our hearts as soon as we act upon it." She understood that whenever we worship God with our hearts and our minds, we are blessed by our love for Him and His love for us.

Loving Him means the thankful acceptance of all things that His love has appointed.

Elisabeth Elliot

—TODAY'S PRAYER—

Dear Heavenly Father, You have blessed me with a love that is infinite and eternal. Let me love You, Lord, more and more each day. Make me a loving servant, Father, today and throughout eternity. And, let me show my love for You by sharing Your message and Your love with others. Amen

MONEY

For the love of money is a root of all sorts of evil, and some by longing for it have wandered away from the faith and pierced themselves with many griefs.

1 Timothy 6:10 NASB

Our society is in love with money and the things that money can buy. God is not. God cares about people, not possessions, and so must we. We must, to the best of our abilities, love our neighbors as ourselves, and we must, to the best of our abilities, resist the mighty temptation to place possessions ahead of people.

Money, in and of itself, is not evil; worshipping money is. So today, as you prioritize matters of importance for you and yours, remember that God is almighty, but the dollar is not. If we worship God, we are blessed. But if we worship "the almighty dollar," we are inevitably punished because of our misplaced priorities—and our punishment inevitably comes sooner rather than later.

—TODAY'S PRAYER—

Dear Lord, help make me a responsible steward of my financial resources. Let me trust Your Holy Word, and let me use my tithe for the support of Your church and for the eternal glory of Your Son. Amen

HIS PEACE

God has called us to peace.

1 Corinthians 7:15 NKJV

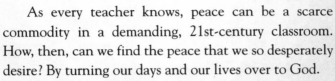

As every teacher knows, peace can be a scarce commodity in a demanding, 21st-century classroom. How, then, can we find the peace that we so desperately desire? By turning our days and our lives over to God.

The beautiful words of John 14:27 give us hope: "Peace I leave with you, my peace I give unto you . . . ." Jesus offers us peace, not as the world gives, but as He alone gives. We, as believers, can accept His peace or ignore it. When we accept God's peace, we are blessed; when we ignore it, we suffer bitter consequences.

Today, as a gift to yourself, to your family, and to your students, claim the inner peace that is your spiritual birthright: the peace of Jesus Christ. It is offered freely; it has been paid for in full; it is yours for the asking. So ask. And then share.

Now God designed the human machine to run on Himself. God cannot give us happiness and peace apart from Himself, because it is not there. There is no such thing.

C. S. Lewis

THE POWER OF PRAYER

For the eyes of the Lord are over the righteous, and his ears are open unto their prayers: but the face of the Lord is against them that do evil.

1 Peter 3:12 KJV

"The power of prayer": these words are so familiar, yet sometimes, we forget what they mean. Prayer is a powerful tool for communicating with our Creator; it is an opportunity to commune with the Giver of all things good. Prayer helps us find strength for today and hope for the future. Prayer is a tool we can use to help others. Prayer is not a thing to be taken lightly or to be used infrequently.

Is prayer an integral part of your life, or is it a hit-or-miss habit? Do you "pray without ceasing," or is your prayer life an afterthought? Do you regularly pray for your family, your friends, and your students . . . or do you bow your head only when others are watching?

The quality of your spiritual life will be in direct proportion to the quality of your prayer life. Prayer changes things, and it changes you. Today, instead of turning things over in your mind, turn them over to God in prayer. Instead of worrying about your next decision, ask God to lead the way. Don't limit your prayers to meals or to bedtime. Pray constantly about things great and small. God is listening, and He wants to hear from you now.

FRESH OPPORTUNITIES

But those who trust in the Lord will renew their strength; they will soar on wings like eagles; they will run and not grow weary; they will walk and not faint.

Isaiah 40:31 Holman CSB

Each new day offers countless opportunities to celebrate life and to serve God's children. But each day also offers countless opportunities to fall prey to the countless distractions of our difficult age.

Consider this day a new beginning. Consider it a fresh start, a renewed opportunity to serve your friends and family with willing hands and a loving heart.

Gigi Graham Tchividjian observed, "How much of our lives are, well, so daily. How often our hours are filled with the mundane, seemingly unimportant things that have to be done, whether at home or work. These very 'daily' tasks could—and should—become a celebration."

Make your life a celebration. After all, your talents are unique, as are your opportunities. So the best time to really live—and really celebrate—is now.

Walking with God leads to receiving his intimate counsel, and counseling leads to deep restoration.

John Eldredge

A LIFE OF SERVICE

So prepare your minds for service and have self-control. All your hope should be for the gift of grace that will be yours when Jesus Christ is shown to you.

1 Peter 1:13 NCV

As a teacher, you have chosen a life of service. Congratulations. Jesus teaches that the most esteemed men and women are not the political leaders or the captains of industry. To the contrary, Jesus teaches that the greatest among us are those who choose to minister and to serve.

When you decided to become a teacher, you demonstrated your willingness to serve in a very tangible way. As a result, you can be comforted by the knowledge that your kindness and generosity will touch the lives of students in ways that you may never fully comprehend. But God knows the impact of your good works, and He will bless you because of them.

The words of Galatians 6:9 are clear: "Let us not become weary in doing good, for at the proper time we will reap a harvest if we do not give up" (NIV). May you never grow weary of your role as a teacher, and may your good works continue to bless your students long after the final school bell has rung.

STRENGTH

Be alert, stand firm in the faith, be brave and strong.
1 Corinthians 16:13 Holman CSB

If you're a teacher with too many obligations and too few hours in which to meet them, you are not alone: yours is a demanding profession. As a dedicated teacher, you may experience moments when you feel overworked, overstressed, and under-appreciated. Thankfully, God stands ready to renew your optimism and your strength if you turn to Him.

When you feel worried or weary, focus your thoughts upon God and upon His love for you. Then, ask Him for the wisdom to prioritize your life and the strength to fulfill your responsibilities. God will give you the energy to do the most important things on today's to-do list . . . if you ask Him. So ask Him.

—TODAY'S PRAYER—

Lord, sometimes life is difficult. Sometimes, I am worried, weary, or heartbroken. But, when I lift my eyes to You, Father, You strengthen me. When I am weak, You lift me up. Today, I turn to You, Lord, for my strength, for my hope, and my salvation. Amen

ACTIONS AND BELIEFS

Who is wise and understanding among you? He should show his works by good conduct with wisdom's gentleness.

James 3:13 Holman CSB

English clergyman Thomas Fuller observed, "He does not believe who does not live according to his beliefs." These words are most certainly true. We may proclaim our beliefs to our hearts' content, but our proclamations will mean nothing—to others or to ourselves—unless we accompany our words with deeds that match. The sermons that we live are far more compelling than the ones we preach.

Like it or not, your life is an accurate reflection of your creed. If this fact gives you some cause for concern, don't bother talking about the changes that you intend to make—make them. And then, when your good deeds speak for themselves—as they most certainly will—don't interrupt.

—TODAY'S PRAYER—

Dear Lord, I have heard Your Word, and I have felt Your presence in my heart; let me act accordingly. Let my words and deeds serve as a testimony to the changes You have made in my life. Let me praise You, Father, by following in the footsteps of Your Son. Amen

YOUR GOOD WORKS

Therefore as you have received Christ Jesus the Lord, walk in Him.

Colossians 2:6 Holman CSB

When we seek righteousness in our own lives—and when we seek the companionship of those who do likewise—we reap the spiritual rewards that God intends for us to enjoy. When we behave ourselves as godly men and women, we honor God. When we live righteously and according to God's commandments, He blesses us in ways that we cannot fully understand.

Today, as you fulfill your responsibilities, hold fast to that which is good, and associate yourself with believers who behave themselves in a like fashion. When you do, your good works will serve as powerful examples for others and as a worthy offering to your Creator.

—TODAY'S PRAYER—

Lord, because I am a teacher, I am a role model to my students. I pray that my actions will always be consistent with my beliefs. I know that my deeds speak more loudly than my words. May every step that I take reflect Your truth and love, and may others be drawn to You because of my words and my deeds. Amen

TOO BUSY?

Don't burn out; keep yourselves fueled and aflame. Be alert servants of the Master, cheerfully expectant. Don't quit in hard times; pray all the harder.

Romans 12:11-12 MSG

Has the busy pace of life robbed you of the peace that might otherwise be yours through Jesus Christ? If so, you are simply too busy for your own good. Through His Son Jesus, God offers you a peace that passes human understanding, but He won't force His peace upon you; in order to experience it, you must slow down long enough to sense His presence and His love.

Today, as a gift to yourself, to your family, and to the world, slow down and claim the inner peace that is your spiritual birthright: the peace of Jesus Christ. It is offered freely; it has been paid for in full; it is yours for the asking. So ask. And then share.

In our tense, uptight society where folks are rushing to make appointments they have already missed, a good laugh can be a refreshing as a cup of cold water in the desert.

Barbara Johnson

LOVE WITHOUT LIMITS

I am the good shepherd. The good shepherd lays down his life for the sheep.

John 10:11 Holman CSB

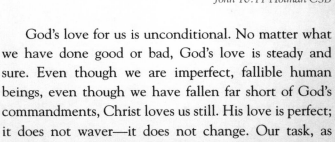

God's love for us is unconditional. No matter what we have done good or bad, God's love is steady and sure. Even though we are imperfect, fallible human beings, even though we have fallen far short of God's commandments, Christ loves us still. His love is perfect; it does not waver—it does not change. Our task, as believers, is to accept Christ's love and to encourage others to do likewise.

In today's troubled world, we all need the love and the peace that is found through the Son of God. Thankfully, Christ's love has no limits. We, in turn, should love Him with no limits, beginning now and ending never.

—TODAY'S PRAYER—

Thank You, Lord, for Your Son. His love is boundless, infinite, and eternal. Today, let me pause and reflect upon Christ's love for me, and let me share that love with all those who cross my path. And, as an expression of my love for Him, let me share Christ's saving message with a world that desperately needs His grace. Amen

GENUINE CONTENTMENT

Your life should be free from the love of money. Be satisfied with what you have, for He Himself has said, I will never leave you or forsake you.

Hebrews 13:5 Holman CSB

Where can we find contentment? Is it a result of wealth, or power, or beauty, or fame? Hardly. Genuine contentment is a gift from God to those who trust Him and follow His commandments.

Our modern world seems preoccupied with the search for happiness. We are bombarded with messages telling us that happiness depends upon the acquisition of material possessions. These messages are false. Enduring peace is not the result of our acquisitions; it is a spiritual gift from God to those who obey Him and accept His will.

If we don't find contentment in God, we will never find it anywhere else. But, if we seek Him and obey Him, we will be blessed with an inner peace: His peace. When God dwells at the center of our lives, contentment will belong to us just as surely as we belong to God.

Real contentment hinges on what's happening inside us, not around us.

Charles Stanley

NOT CRUSHED

We are pressured in every way but not crushed; we are perplexed but not in despair.

2 Corinthians 4:8 Holman CSB

Throughout the seasons of life, we must all endure life-altering personal losses that leave us breathless. When we do, God stands ready to protect us. Psalm 147 promises, "He heals the brokenhearted, and binds their wounds" (v. 3 NASB). And God keeps His promises.

Life is often challenging, but as Christians, we must trust the promises of our Heavenly Father. God loves us, and He will protect us. In times of hardship, He will comfort us; in times of sorrow, He will dry our tears. When we are troubled, or weak, or sorrowful, God is with us. His love endures, not only for today, but also for all of eternity.

Underneath each trouble there is a faithful purpose.

C. H. Spurgeon

—TODAY'S PRAYER—

Deal Lord, in these difficult days, let me trust the wisdom that I find in Your Holy Word. I seek wisdom, Lord, not as the world gives, but as You give. Lead me in Your ways so that, in time, my wisdom might glorify Your kingdom and Your Son. Amen

BIG PLANS

With God's power working in us, God can do much, much more than anything we can ask or imagine.

Ephesians 3:20 NCV

Are you willing to entertain the possibility that God has big plans in store for you as well as your students? Hopefully so. Yet sometimes, especially if you've recently experienced a life-altering disappointment, you may find it difficult to envision the possibility of a brighter future. If so, it's time to stop placing limitations upon yourself, upon your students, and upon God.

It takes courage to dream big dreams. You will discover that courage when you do three things: accept the past, trust God to handle the future, and make the most of the time He has given you today.

Nothing is too difficult for God, and no dreams are too big for Him—not even yours. So start living—and dreaming—accordingly.

—TODAY'S PRAYER—

Dear Lord, give me the courage to dream and the wisdom to help my students do likewise. When I am worried or weary, give me strength for today and hope for tomorrow. Keep me mindful of Your miraculous power, Your infinite love, and Your eternal salvation. Amen

POWERFUL EXAMPLES

You should be an example to the believers in speech, in conduct, in love, in faith, in purity.

1 Timothy 4:12 Holman CSB

We are all teachers: all of us serve as powerful examples to young people, friends, and family members. And we must behave accordingly.

God has placed people along your path, people whom He intends for you to influence. Every time you serve as a positive example, you help to reshape the world and to refashion eternity.

More depends on my walk than my talk.

D. L. Moody

In your desire to share the gospel, you may be the only Jesus someone else will ever meet. Be real and be involved with people.

Barbara Johnson

—TODAY'S PRAYER—

Lord, make me a worthy example to my family and friends. And, let my words and my deeds serve as a testimony to the changes You have made in my life. Let me praise You, Father, by following in the footsteps of Your Son, and let others see Him through me. Amen

FAMILY

Unless the Lord builds a house, its builders labor over it in vain; unless the Lord watches over a city, the watchman stays alert in vain.

Psalm 127:1 HSCB

In the life of every family, there are moments of frustration and disappointment. Lots of them. But, for those who are lucky enough to live in the presence of a close-knit, caring clan, the rewards far outweigh the frustrations.

No family is perfect, and neither is yours. But, despite the inevitable challenges and hurt feelings of family life, your clan is God's gift to you. That little band of men, women, kids, and babies is a priceless treasure on temporary loan from the Father above. Give thanks to the Giver for the gift of family…and act accordingly.

Make sure your house is prayer-conditioned.

Anonymous

—TODAY'S PRAYER—

Father, help me to treasure those moments that I spend with my family—and let me demonstrate, through my words and my actions, how much love I feel in my heart for them. Amen

FOLLOWING CHRIST

Therefore as you have received Christ Jesus the Lord, walk in Him.

Colossians 2:6 Holman CSB

Hannah Whitall Smith spoke to believers of every generation when she advised, "Keep your face upturned to Christ as the flowers do to the sun. Look, and your soul shall live and grow." That's powerful advice. When we turn our hearts to Jesus, we receive His blessings, His peace, and His grace.

Do you regularly take time each day to embrace Christ's love? Do you prayerfully ask God to lead you in the footsteps of His Son? And are you determined to obey God's Word even if the world encourages you to do otherwise? If so, you'll soon experience of the peace and the power that flows freely from the Son of God.

We have in Jesus Christ a perfect example of how to put God's truth into practice.

Bill Bright

—TODAY'S PRAYER—

Dear Jesus, because I am Your disciple, I will trust You, I will obey Your teachings, and I will share Your Good News. You have given me life abundant and life eternal, and I will follow You today and forever. Amen

UNFOLDING PLANS

What a God we have! And how fortunate we are to have him, this Father of our Master Jesus! Because Jesus was raised from the dead, we've been given a brand-new life and have everything to live for, including a future in heaven—and the future starts now!

1 Peter 1:3-4 MSG

As you consider God's unfolding plans for your life, you will undoubtedly look to the future . . . after all, the future is where those plans will take place. But sometimes, the future may seem foreboding indeed.

In these uncertain times, it's easy to lose faith in the possibility of a better tomorrow . . . but it's wrong. God instructs us to trust His wisdom, His plan, and His love. When we do so, the future becomes a glorious opportunity to help others, to praise our Creator, and to share God's Good News.

Today, as you stand before your classroom, help your students face the future with optimism, hope, and self-confidence. After all, even in these uncertain times, God still has the last word. And His love endures to all generations, including this one.

Don't ever forget there are more firsts to come.

Dennis Swanberg

HIS LOVE FOR YOU

The unfailing love of the Lord never ends!

Lamentations 3:22 NLT

St. Augustine observed, "God loves each of us as if there were only one of us." Do you believe those words? Do you seek to have an intimate, one-on-one relationship with your Heavenly Father, or are you satisfied to keep Him at a "safe" distance?

Sometimes, in the crush of our daily duties, God may seem far away, but He is not. God is everywhere we have ever been and everywhere we will ever go. He is with us night and day; He knows our thoughts and our prayers. And, when we earnestly seek Him, we will find Him because He is here, waiting patiently for us to reach out to Him.

Let us reach out to Him today and always. And let us praise Him for the glorious gifts that have transformed us today and forever. Amen.

Being loved by Him whose opinion matters most gives us the security to risk loving, too—even loving ourselves.

Gloria Gaither

HIS WILL

"Father, if it is Your will, take this cup away from Me; nevertheless not My will, but Yours, be done."

Luke 22:42 NKJV

God has a plan for all of our lives. As a teacher, you bear a special responsibility for training the students who are entrusted to your care. Because of your position as a guide and mentor, you must be especially careful to seek God's will and to follow it.

As this day unfolds, seek God's will and obey His Word. When you entrust your life to Him completely and without reservation, He will give you the strength to meet any challenge, the courage to face any trial, and the wisdom to live in His righteousness and in His peace.

God is God. He knows what he is doing. When you can't trace his hand, trust his heart.

Max Lucado

—TODAY'S PRAYER—

Lord, let Your will be my will. When I am confused, give me maturity and wisdom. When I am worried, give me courage and strength. Let me be Your faithful servant, Father, always seeking Your guidance and Your will for my life. Amen

HE FORGIVES COMPLETELY

Be diligent to present yourself approved to God, a worker who doesn't need to be ashamed, correctly teaching the word of truth.

2 Timothy 2:15 Holman CSB

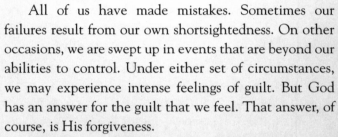

All of us have made mistakes. Sometimes our failures result from our own shortsightedness. On other occasions, we are swept up in events that are beyond our abilities to control. Under either set of circumstances, we may experience intense feelings of guilt. But God has an answer for the guilt that we feel. That answer, of course, is His forgiveness.

When we ask our Heavenly Father for His forgiveness, He forgives us completely and without reservation. Then, we must do the difficult work of forgiving ourselves in the same way that God has forgiven us: thoroughly and unconditionally.

The Spanish writer Baltasar Gracián noted, "The things we remember best are those better forgotten." If those words describe your thoughts, then it's time for a special kind of housecleaning—a housecleaning of your mind and your heart.

Satan knows that if you live under a dark cloud of guilt, you will not be able to witness effectively or serve the Lord with power and blessing.

Warren Wiersbe

HE DOESN'T CHANGE

Jesus Christ is the same yesterday, today, and forever.

Hebrews 13:8 Holman CSB

Our circumstances change but Jesus does not. Even when the world seems to be trembling between our feet, Jesus remains the spiritual bedrock that cannot be moved.

The old familiar hymn begins, "What a friend we have in Jesus…." No truer words were ever penned. Jesus is the sovereign friend and ultimate Savior of mankind. Christ showed enduring love for His believers by willingly sacrificing His own life so that we might have eternal life. Let us love Him, praise Him, and share His message of salvation with our neighbors and with the world.

Jesus was the Savior Who would deliver them not only from the bondage of sin but also from meaningless wandering through life.

Anne Graham Lotz

His name sounds down the corridors of the centuries like the music of all choirs, visible and invisible, poured forth in one anthem.

R. G. Lee

WALKING WITH THE WISE

A wise man will hear and increase learning, and a man of understanding will attain wise counsel.

Proverbs 1:5 NKJV

Do you wish to become a better teacher and a wiser person? Then you must walk with people who, by their words and their presence, make you wiser. But that's not all; you must avoid those people who encourage you to think foolish thoughts or do foolish things.

Today, as a gift to yourself, select, from your friends and coworkers, a mentor whose judgement you trust. Then listen carefully to your mentor's advice and be willing to accept that advice, even if accepting it requires effort, or pain, or both. Consider your mentor to be God's gift to you. Thank God for that gift, and treasure the wisdom that you gain.

And what should you do with all that hard-earned knowledge that you acquire from your mentor? Share it, of course, with the students and coworkers who are wise enough to learn from you.

The effective mentor strives to help a man or woman discover what they can be in Christ and then holds them accountable to become that person.

Howard Hendricks

JOYFUL THOUGHTS

My cup runs over. Surely goodness and mercy shall follow me all the days of my life; and I will dwell in the house of the Lord Forever.

Psalm 23:5-6 NKJV

Christians have every reason to be optimistic about life. As Billy Graham observed, "Christ can put a spring in your step and a thrill in your heart. Optimism and cheerfulness are products of knowing Christ." But sometimes, when we are tired or frustrated, optimism and cheerfulness seem like distant promises. They are not. Thankfully, our God stands ready to restore us: "I will give you a new heart and put a new spirit in you…" (Ezekiel 36:26 NIV). Our task, of course, is to let Him.

Today, accept the new spirit that God seeks to infuse into your heart. Think optimistically about yourself, your students, your school, and your world. Rejoice in this glorious day that the Lord has given you, and share your optimism with your friends, with your coworkers, and with your students. Your enthusiasm will be contagious. And your words will bring healing and comfort to a world that needs both.

It is a remarkable thing that some of the most optimistic and enthusiastic people you will meet are those who have been through intense suffering.

Warren Wiersbe

YOUR TREASURE?

Your heart will be where your treasure is.

Luke 12:34 NCV

On the grand stage of a well-lived life, material possessions should play a rather small role. Of course, we all need the basic necessities of life, but once we meet those needs for ourselves and for our families, the piling up of possessions creates more problems than it solves. Our real riches, of course, are not of this world. We are never really rich until we are rich in spirit.

Do you find yourself wrapped up in the concerns of the material world? If so, it's time to reorder your priorities by turning your thoughts and your prayers to more important matters. And, it's time to begin storing up riches that will endure throughout eternity: the spiritual kind.

We act as though comfort and luxury were the chief requirements of life, when all we need to make us really happy is something to be enthusiastic about.

Charles Kingsley

Great wealth is not related to money! It is an attitude of satisfaction coupled with inner peace.

Charles Swindoll

LIVING ON PURPOSE

I urge you to live a life worthy of the calling you have received.

Ephesians 4:1 NIV

Life is best lived on purpose, not by accident—the sooner we discover what God intends for us to do with our lives, the better. But the search to find meaning and purpose for our lives is seldom easy. Sometimes, we wander aimlessly in a wilderness of our own making. And sometimes, we must try—and fail—many times before we discover our life's work.

Mother Teresa observed, "We are all pencils in the hand of God." And Willa Cather noted "This is happiness: to be dissolved in something complete and great." How true.

Today is a wonderful day to "dissolve yourself" in something important. You can do it—and if you get busy, you will.

—TODAY'S PRAYER—

Dear Lord, let Your purposes be my purposes. Let Your priorities be my priorities. Let Your will be my will. Let Your Word be my guide. And, let me grow in faith and in wisdom today and every day. Amen

FACING YOUR FEARS

But when Jesus heard it, He answered him, "Don't be afraid. Only believe."

Luke 8:50 Holman CSB

Do you prefer to face your fears rather than run from them? If so, you will be blessed because of your willingness to live courageously.

When Paul wrote Timothy, he reminded his young protégé that the God they served was a bold God, and God's spirit empowered His children with boldness also. Like Timothy, we face times of uncertainty and fear. God's message is the same to us, today, as it was to Timothy: We can live boldly because the spirit of God resides in us.

So today, as you face the challenges of everyday living, remember that God is with you . . . and you are protected.

Faith is stronger than fear.

John Maxwell

—TODAY'S PRAYER—

Dear Lord, when I am called upon to face my fears, give me courage. Let my words and deeds be pleasing to You, and let my actions be worthy of the One who sacrificed His life for mine. Amen

MEASURED WORDS

Be gracious in your speech. The goal is to bring out the best in others in a conversation, not put them down, not cut them out.

Colossians 4:6 MSG

All too often, we underestimate the importance of the words we speak. Whether we realize it or not, our words carry great weight and great power. If our words are encouraging, we can lift others up; if our words are hurtful, we can hold others back.

The Bible reminds us that "Reckless words pierce like a sword, but the tongue of the wise brings healing" (Proverbs 12:18 NIV). In other words, if we are to solve more problems than we start, we must measure our words carefully.

Do you seek to be a source of encouragement to others? And, do you seek to be a worthy ambassador for Christ? If so, you must speak words that are worthy of your Savior. So think before you speak. Avoid angry outbursts. Refrain from constant criticism. Terminate tantrums. Negate negativism. Cease from being cynical. Instead, use Christ as your guide, and speak words of encouragement and hope to a world that needs both.

Change the heart, and you change the speech.

Warren Wiersbe

COMPASSION

Finally, all of you be of one mind, having compassion for one another; love as brothers, be tenderhearted, be courteous.

1 Peter 3:8 NKJV

God's Word commands us to be compassionate, generous servants to those who need our support. As believers, we have been richly blessed by our Creator. We, in turn, are called to share our gifts, our possessions, our testimonies, and our talents.

The thread of compassion is woven into the very fabric of Christ's teachings. If we are to be disciples of Christ, we, too, must be zealous in caring for others. Our Savior expects no less from us. And He deserves no less.

We must learn to regard people less in the light of what they do or do not do, and more in the light of what they suffer.

Dietrich Bonhoeffer

—TODAY'S PRAYER—

Lord, make me a loving, encouraging, compassionate Christian. And, let my love for Christ be reflected through the kindness that I show to my family, to my friends, and to all who need the healing touch of the Master's hand. Amen

CELEBRATION

Rejoice in the Lord always. I will say it again: Rejoice!
Philippians 4:4 Holman CSB

Do you approach each day with celebration or with reservation? If you are a believer who has been redeemed by a loving Savior, the answer should be obvious. Each day should be a cause for celebration and for praise.

Thoughtful Christians should be joyful Christians. And even on life's darker days, even during those difficult times when we scarcely see a single ray of sunlight, we can still praise God and thank Him for our blessings. When we do, we demonstrate that our acquaintance with the Master is not a passing fancy but is, instead, the cornerstone and the touchstone of our lives.

If you can forgive the person you were, accept the person you are, and believe in the person you will become, you are headed for joy. So celebrate your life.

Barbara Johnson

—TODAY'S PRAYER—

Dear Lord, let me celebrate this moment and every moment of life. Let me celebrate You and Your marvelous creation, Father, and let me give thanks for this day. Today is Your gift to me, Lord. Let me use it to Your glory while giving all the praise to You. Amen

THE WORK OF TEACHING

Remember: A stingy planter gets a stingy crop; a lavish planter gets a lavish crop.

2 Corinthians 9:6 MSG

Being a teacher is not an easy job. The demands and pressures of the classroom, combined with late-night paper-grading marathons and lesson preparations, can leave even the most experienced teacher feeling overworked and under appreciated. Thankfully, teaching is not only a difficult job, it is also a highly rewarding one.

As a teacher, you have countless opportunities to do great things for God. So it's no surprise that the teaching profession is sometimes difficult. Reaching for great things usually requires work and lots of it, which is perfectly fine with God. After all, He knows that you're up to the task, and He has big plans for you and for your students. Very big plans . . .

—TODAY'S PRAYER—

Dear Lord, make my work pleasing to You. Help me to sow the seeds of Your abundance in the classroom and everywhere I go. Let me be diligent in all my undertakings and give me patience to wait for Your harvest. Amen

JUDGE NOT

Judge not, and you shall not be judged. Condemn not, and you shall not be condemned. Forgive, and you will be forgiven.

Luke 6:37 NKJV

The warning of Matthew 7:1 is clear: "Judge not, that ye be not judged" (KJV). Yet even the most devoted Christians may fall prey to a powerful yet subtle temptation: the temptation to judge others. But as obedient followers of Christ, we are commanded to refrain from such behavior.

As Jesus came upon a young woman who had been condemned by the Pharisees, He spoke not only to the crowd that was gathered there, but also to all generations when He warned, "He that is without sin among you, let him first cast a stone at her" (John 8:7 KJV). Christ's message is clear, and it applies not only to the Pharisees of ancient times, but also to us.

Judging draws the judgment of others.

Catherine Marshall

Christians think they are prosecuting attorneys or judges, when, in reality, God has called all of us to be witnesses.

Warren Wiersbe

HE GUIDES AND PROTECTS

The LORD is my strength and song, and He has become my salvation.

Exodus 15:2 NASB

God has promised to lift you up and guide your steps if you let Him do so. God has promised that when you entrust your life to Him completely and without reservation, He will give you the strength to meet any challenge, the courage to face any trial, and the wisdom to live in His righteousness.

God's hand uplifts those who turn their hearts and prayers to Him. Will you count yourself among that number? Will you accept God's peace and wear God's armor against the temptations and distractions of our dangerous world? If you do, you can live courageously and optimistically, knowing that you have been forever touched by the loving, unfailing, uplifting hand of God.

Our life is full of brokenness—bitter relationships, broken promises, broken expectations. How can we live with that brokenness without becoming bitter and resentful except by returning again and again to God's faithful presence in our lives?

Henri Nouwen

THE FAITHFUL SERVANT

His master said to him, "Well done, good and faithful slave!
You were faithful over a few things; I will put you in charge
of many things. Enter your master's joy!"

Matthew 25:21 Holman CSB

The Bible teaches us about the abundance that can be ours through Christ. But what, exactly, did Jesus mean when He promised "life...more abundantly"? Was He referring to material possessions or financial wealth? Hardly. Jesus offers a different kind of abundance: a spiritual richness that extends beyond the temporal boundaries of this world. This everlasting abundance is available to all who seek it and claim it. May we, as believers, claim the riches of Christ Jesus every day that we live, and may we share His blessings with our students, with our families, with our coworkers, and with the world.

—TODAY'S PRAYER—

Heavenly Father, You have promised an abundant life through Your Son Jesus. Thank You, Lord, for Your abundance. Guide me according to Your will, so that I might be a worthy servant in all that I say and do, this day and every day. Amen

ASK HIM

He granted their request because they trusted in Him.
1 Chronicles 5:20 Holman CSB

Sometimes, amid the demands and the frustrations of everyday life, we forget to slow ourselves down long enough to talk with God. Instead of turning our thoughts and prayers to Him, we rely upon our own resources. Instead of praying for strength and courage, we seek to manufacture it within ourselves. Instead of asking God for guidance, we depend only upon our own limited wisdom. The results of such behaviors are unfortunate and, on occasion, tragic.

Are you in need? Ask God to sustain you. Are you troubled? Take your worries to Him in prayer. Are you weary? Seek God's strength. In all things great and small, seek God's wisdom and His grace. He hears your prayers, and He will answer. All you must do is ask.

If we do not have hearts that call out to him, we forfeit the deliverance. "You do not have, because you do not ask God" (James 4:2 NIV) is probably the saddest commentary on any life, especially the life of a Christian.

Jim Cymbala

BLESSINGS

I will send down showers in their season—showers of blessing.

Ezekiel 34:26 Holman CSB

Have you counted your blessings lately? You should. Of course, God's gifts are too numerous to count, but as a grateful Christian, you should attempt to count them nonetheless.

Your blessings include life, family, friends, career, talents, and possessions, for starters. And your greatest gift—a treasure that was paid for on the cross and is yours for the asking—is God's gift of salvation through Christ Jesus.

Think of the blessings we so easily take for granted: Life itself; preservation from danger; every bit of health we enjoy; every hour of liberty; the ability to see, to hear, to speak, to think, and to imagine all this comes from the hand of God.

Billy Graham

Count your blessings! Recounts are OK . . .

Anonymous

CHEERFUL?

Be cheerful. Keep things in good repair. Keep your spirits up. Think in harmony. Be agreeable. Do all that, and the God of love and peace will be with you for sure.

2 Corinthians 13:11 MSG

Oswald Chambers correctly observed, "Joy is the great note all throughout the Bible." He might have added that joy should also be the cornerstone of learning. Today, let us celebrate life as God intended. Today, let us put smiles on our faces, kind words on our lips, and songs in our hearts. And, while we're at it, let's infuse as much joy as we can into the classroom. God loves a cheerful giver and a cheerful teacher.

God is good, and heaven is forever. And if those two facts don't cheer you up, nothing will.

Marie T. Freeman

—TODAY'S PRAYER—

Dear Lord, You have given me so many reasons to celebrate. Today, let me choose an attitude of cheerfulness. Let me be a joyful Christian, Lord, quick to smile and slow to anger. And, let me share Your goodness with all whom I meet so that Your love might shine in me and through me. Amen

GOOD COMMUNICATION

A gentle answer turns away anger, but a harsh word stirs up wrath.

Proverbs 15:1 Holman CSB

If you seek to be a source of encouragement to friends, to family members and to coworkers, then you must measure your words carefully. And that's exactly what God wants you to do. God's Word reminds us that "Reckless words pierce like a sword, but the tongue of the wise brings healing" (Proverbs 12:18 NIV).

Today, make this promise to yourself: vow to be an honest, effective, encouraging communicator at work, at home, and everyplace in between. Speak wisely, not impulsively. Use words of kindness and praise, not words of anger or derision. Learn how to be truthful without being cruel. Remember that you have the power to heal others or to injure them, to lift others up or to hold them back. And when you learn how to lift them up, you'll soon discover that you've lifted yourself up, too.

Part of good communication is listening with the eyes as well as with the ears.

Josh McDowell

CRITICISM

Don't criticize one another, brothers. He who criticizes a brother or judges his brother criticizes the law and judges the law. But if you judge the law, you are not a doer of the law but a judge.

James 4:11 Holman CSB

From experience, we know that it is easier to criticize than to correct. And we know that it is easier to find faults than solutions. Yet, the urge to criticize others remains a powerful temptation for most of us. Our task, as obedient believers, is to break the twin habits of negative thinking and critical speech.

Negativity is highly contagious: we give it to others who, in turn, give it back to us. This cycle can be broken by positive thoughts, heartfelt prayers, and encouraging words. As thoughtful servants of a loving God, we can use the transforming power of Christ's love to break the chains of negativity. And we should.

—TODAY'S PRAYER—

Help me, Lord, rise above the need to criticize others. May my own shortcomings humble me, and may I always be a source of genuine encouragement to my family and friends. Amen

DISCIPLINE YOURSELF

*But have nothing to do with irreverent and silly myths.
Rather, train yourself in godliness.*

1 Timothy 4:7 Holman CSB

God's Word is clear: as believers, we are called to lead lives of discipline, diligence, moderation, and maturity. But the world often tempts us to behave otherwise. Everywhere we turn, or so it seems, we are faced with powerful temptations to behave in undisciplined, ungodly ways.

God's Word instructs us to be disciplined in our thoughts and our actions; God's Word warns us against the dangers of impulsive behavior. As believers in a just God, we should think and react accordingly.

If one examines the secret behind a championship football team, a magnificent orchestra, or a successful business, the principal ingredient is invariably discipline.

James Dobson

—TODAY'S PRAYER—

Dear Lord, I want to be a disciplined believer. Let me use my time wisely, let me obey Your commandments faithfully, and let me worship You joyfully, today and every day. Amen

ENERGY

Be energetic in your life of salvation, reverent and sensitive before God. That energy is God's energy, an energy deep within you, God himself willing and working at what will give him the most pleasure.

Philippians 2:12-13 MSG

Are you fired with enthusiasm for Christ? If so, congratulations, and keep up the good work! But, if your spiritual batteries are running low, then perhaps you're spending too much energy working for yourself and not enough energy working for God.

We mortals are at our best when we give. Some of us try desperately to hold on to ourselves, to live for ourselves. But giving is our nature, and we are never fully at peace unless we are faithfully living in accordance with God's will for our lives. God's instructions are clear. As believers, we are to be generous, enthusiastic stewards of the talents and energies that God has bestowed upon us.

Are you an energized Christian? You should be. But if you're not, you must seek strength and renewal from the one source that will never fail: that source, of course, is your Heavenly Father. And rest assured—when you sincerely petition Him, He will give you all the strength you need to live victoriously for Him.

FAITH

Now without faith it is impossible to please God, for the one who draws near to Him must believe that He exists and rewards those who seek Him.

Hebrews 11:6 Holman CSB

The first element of a successful life is faith: faith in God, faith in His Son, and faith in His promises. If we place our lives in God's hands, our faith is rewarded in ways that we—as human beings with clouded vision and limited understanding—can scarcely comprehend. But, if we seek to rely solely upon our own resources, or if we seek earthly success outside the boundaries of God's commandments, we reap a bitter harvest for ourselves and for our loved ones.

Do you desire the abundance and success that God has promised? Then trust Him today and every day that you live. Trust Him with every aspect of your life. Trust His promises, and trust in the saving grace of His only begotten Son. Then, when you have entrusted your future to the Giver of all things good, rest assured that your future is secure, not only for today, but also for all eternity.

Faith in faith is pointless. Faith in a living, active God moves mountains.

Beth Moore

A HEALTHY FEAR

The fear of the Lord is a fountain of life, turning people from the snares of death.

Proverbs 14:27 Holman CSB

Do you have a healthy, fearful respect for God's power? If so, you are both wise and obedient. And, because you are a thoughtful believer, you also understand that genuine wisdom begins with a profound appreciation for God's limitless power.

God praises humility and punishes pride. That's why God's greatest servants will always be those humble men and women who care less for their own glory and more for God's glory. In God's kingdom, the only way to achieve greatness is to shun it. And the only way to be wise is to understand these facts: God is great; He is all-knowing; and He is all-powerful. We must respect Him, and we must humbly obey His commandments, or we must accept the consequences of our misplaced pride.

—TODAY'S PRAYER—

Dear Lord, let my greatest fear be the fear of displeasing You. I will strive, Father, to obey Your commandments and seek Your will this day and every day of my life. Amen

FORGIVENESS AND RENEWAL

Praise the Lord, I tell myself, and never forget the good things he does for me. He forgives all my sins and heals all my diseases.

Psalm 103:3 NLT

Bitterness saps your energy; genuine forgiveness renews your spirit. If you find yourself tired, discouraged, or worse, perhaps you need to ask God to help you forgive others (just as He has already forgiven you).

God intends that His children lead joyous lives filled with abundance and peace. But sometimes, abundance and peace seem very far away. It is in these dark moments that we must turn to God for renewal; when we do, He will restore us.

Are you embittered about the past? Turn your heart toward God in prayer. Are you spiritually depleted? Call upon fellow believers to support you, and call upon Christ to renew your spirit and your life. Do you sincerely want to forgive someone? Ask God to heal your heart. When you do, you'll discover that the Creator of the universe stands always ready and always able to create a new sense of wonderment and joy in you.

But perhaps all peacemaking must begin in a similar spot—in prayer to God, interceding for another, asking blessing for the one who has cursed us, and opening our own hearts for godly examination.

Debra Evans

SPECIAL GIFTS

Now there are different gifts, but the same Spirit. There are different ministries, but the same Lord.

1 Corinthians 12:4-5 Holman CSB

All teachers possess special gifts—bestowed from the Father above—and you are no exception. Yet God's gifts are no guarantee of success; those gifts must be cultivated and nurtured; otherwise they diminish over time.

Perhaps you are one of those lucky teachers who has a natural gift for leading a class. But, even if you have the oratorical skills of Churchill and the mind of Einstein, you can still improve your teaching skills…and you should.

Today, accept this challenge: value the unique gift that God has given you—then, nourish your gift, make it grow, and share it with your students and with the world. After all, the best way to say "Thank You" for God's gift is, quite simply, to use it.

—TODAY'S PRAYER—

Dear Lord, let me use my gifts, and let me help my students discover theirs. Your gifts are priceless and eternal. May we, Your children, use them to the glory of Your kingdom, today and forever. Amen

HIS GUIDEBOOK

For this is the love of God, that we keep His commandments.
And His commandments are not burdensome.

1 John 5:3 NKJV

God has given us a guidebook for righteous living called the Holy Bible. It contains thorough instructions which, if followed, lead to abundance and eternal life. But, if we choose to ignore God's commandments, the results are as predictable as they are tragic. Let us follow God's commandments, and let us conduct our lives in such a way that we might be shining examples for those who have not yet found Christ.

Bible history is filled with people who began the race with great success but failed at the end because they disregarded God's rules.

Warren Wiersbe

It takes faith to obey God, but God always rewards obedient faith.

Warren Wiersbe

—TODAY'S PRAYER—

Thank You, Dear Lord, for loving me enough to give me rules to live by. As I live by Your commandments, let me lead others to do the same. Give me the wisdom to walk righteously in Your way, Dear Lord, trusting always in You. Amen

GOD'S POWER

For His divine power has given us everything required for life and godliness, through the knowledge of Him who called us by His own glory and goodness.

2 Peter 1:3 Holman CSB

Because God's power is limitless, it is far beyond the comprehension of mortal minds. But even though we cannot fully understand the awesome heart of God, we can praise it, worship it, and marvel at its mercy.

God's ability to love is not burdened by boundaries or by limitations. The love that flows from the awesome heart of God is infinite—and today presents yet another opportunity to celebrate His love.

When we worship God with faith and assurance, when we place Him at the absolute center of our lives, we invite His love into our hearts. In turn, we grow to love Him more deeply as we sense His love for us. St. Augustine wrote, "I love you, Lord, not doubtingly, but with absolute certainty. Your Word beat upon my heart until I fell in love with you, and now the universe and everything in it tells me to love you." Let us pray that we, too, will turn our hearts to the Creator, knowing with certainty that His awesome heart has ample room for each of us, and that we, in turn, must make room in our hearts for Him.

GRATITUDE

Everything created by God is good, and nothing is to be rejected, if it is received with gratitude; for it is sanctified by means of the word of God and prayer.

1 Timothy 4:4-5 NASB

For most of us, life is busy and complicated. And, as teachers, we have countless responsibilities that begin long before the school bell rings and end long after the last student has left the classroom. Amid the rush and crush of the daily grind, it is easy to lose sight of God and His blessings. But, when we forget to slow down and say "Thank You" to our Maker, we rob ourselves of His presence, His peace, and His joy. Instead of ignoring God, we should praise Him many times each day. Then, with gratitude in our hearts, we can face the day's complications with the perspective and power that only He can provide.

—TODAY'S PRAYER—

Lord, let my attitude be one of gratitude. You have given me much; when I think of Your grace and goodness, I am humbled and thankful. Today, let me express my thanksgiving, Father, not just through my words but also through my deeds . . . and may all the glory be Yours. Amen

HUMILITY

He has told you men what is good and what it is the Lord requires of you: Only to act justly, to love faithfulness, and to walk humbly with your God.

Micah 6:8 Holman CSB

God's Word clearly instructs us to be humble. And that's good because, as fallible human beings, we have so very much to be humble about! Yet some of us continue to puff ourselves up, seeming to say, "Look at me!" To do so is wrong.

As Christians, we have been refashioned and saved by Jesus Christ, and that salvation came not because of our own good works but because of God's grace. How, then, can we be prideful? The answer, of course, is that, if we are honest with ourselves and with our God, we simply can't be boastful...we must, instead, be eternally grateful and exceedingly humble. The good things in our lives, including our loved ones, come from God. He deserves the credit—and we deserve the glorious experience of giving it to Him.

Because Christ Jesus came to the world clothed in humility, he will always be found among those who are clothed with humility. He will be found among the humble people.

A. W. Tozer

STILL LEARNING

A wise man will listen and increase his learning, and a discerning man will obtain guidance.

Proverbs 1:5 Holman CSB

As long as we live, we should continue to learn. And we should encourage our students to do likewise.

Education is the tool by which we come to know and appreciate the world in which we live. It is the shining light that snuffs out the darkness of ignorance and poverty. Education is freedom just as surely as ignorance is a form of bondage. Education is not a luxury, it is a necessity and a powerful tool for good in this world.

Knowledge can be found in textbooks. Wisdom, on the other hand, is found in God's Holy Word and in the carefully chosen words of loving parents and thoughtful teachers. When we give our children the gift of knowledge, we do them a wonderful service. But, when we share the gift of wisdom, we offer a timeless treasure that surpasses knowledge and reshapes eternity. May we continue to seek wisdom—and to share it—as long as God gives us breath.

The wonderful thing about God's schoolroom is that we get to grade our own papers. You see, He doesn't test us so He can learn how well we're doing. He tests us so we can discover how well we're doing.

Charles Swindoll

THE GREATEST OF THESE

Pay all your debts, except the debt of love for others. You can never finish paying that! If you love your neighbor, you will fulfill all the requirements of God's law.

Romans 13:8 NLT

The beautiful words of 1st Corinthians 13 remind us that love is God's commandment: "But now abide faith, hope, love, these three; but the greatest of these is love" (v. 13, NASB). Faith is important, of course. So, too, is hope. But, love is more important still. Christ showed His love for us on the cross, and, as Christians, we are called upon to return Christ's love by sharing it. Today, let us spread Christ's love to our families, friends, and strangers by word and by deed.

Affection is responsible for nine-tenths of whatever solid and durable happiness there is in our natural lives.

C. S. Lewis

—TODAY'S PRAYER—

Lord, You have given me love that is beyond human understanding, and I am Your loving servant. May the love that I feel for You be reflected in the compassion that I show to my family, to my friends, and to all who cross my path. Amen

NEW BEGINNINGS

You are being renewed in the spirit of your minds; you put on the new man, the one created according to God's likeness in righteousness and purity of the truth.

Ephesians 4:23-24 Holman CSB

If we sincerely want to change ourselves for the better, we must start on the inside and work our way out from there. Lasting change doesn't occur "out there"; it occurs "in here." It occurs, not in the shifting sands of our own particular circumstances, but in quiet depths of our own hearts.

Are you in search of a new beginning or, for that matter, a new you? If so, don't expect changing circumstances to miraculously transform you into the person you want to become. Transformation starts with God, and it starts in the silent center of a humble human heart—like yours.

No matter how badly we have failed, we can always get up and begin again. Our God is the God of new beginnings.

Warren Wiersbe

Only joyous love redeems.

Catherine Marshall

A MARATHON

But as for you, be strong; don't be discouraged, for your work has a reward.

2 Chronicles 15:7 Holman CSB

The familiar saying is true: "Life is a marathon, not a sprint." And, the same can be said of the teaching profession. Teaching requires perseverance, especially on those difficult days when the students are in an uproar and the lesson plan is in disarray. But, our Savior, Christ Jesus, finished what He began, and so must we. Sometimes, God answers our prayers with silence, and when He does, we must patiently persevere. In times of trouble, we must seek God through prayer and lean upon His strength. Whatever our problems, He can handle them. Our job is to keep persevering until He does.

Determination and faithfulness are the nails used to build the house of God's dreams.

Barbara Johnson

Battles are won in the trenches, in the grit and grime of courageous determination; they are won day by day in the arena of life.

Charles Swindoll

YOUR POWERFUL TOOL

Rejoice always! Pray constantly. Give thanks in everything, for this is God's will for you in Christ Jesus.

1 Thessalonians 5:16-18 Holman CSB

Prayer is powerful tool for communicating with our Creator; it is an opportunity to commune with the Giver of all things good. Prayer is not a thing to be taken lightly or to be used infrequently. Prayer should never be reserved for mealtimes or for bedtimes; it should be an ever-present focus in our daily lives.

In his first letter to the Thessalonians, Paul wrote, "Rejoice evermore. Pray without ceasing. In every thing give thanks: for this is the will of God in Christ Jesus concerning you" (v. 5:17-18 KJV). Paul's words apply to every Christian of every generation.

Today, instead of turning things over in our minds, let us turn them over to God in prayer. Instead of worrying about our decisions, let's trust God to help us make them. Today, let us pray constantly about things great and small. God is listening, and He wants to hear from us. Now.

You can talk to God because God listens. Even if you stammer or stumble, even if what you have to say impresses no one, it impresses God, and he listens.

Max Lucado

HE RENEWS US

I will give you a new heart and put a new spirit within you.
Ezekiel 36:26 Holman CSB

Today, like every other day, is literally brimming with possibilities. Whether we realize it or not, God is always working in us and through us; our job is to let Him do His work without undue interference. Yet we are imperfect beings who, because of our limited vision, often resist God's will. We want life to unfold according to our own desires, not God's. But, our Heavenly Father may have other plans.

As you begin this new year, think carefully about the work that God can do through you. And then, set out upon the next phase of your life's journey with a renewed sense of purpose and hope. God has the power to make all things new, including you. Your job is to let Him do it.

—TODAY'S PRAYER—

Lord, sometimes, the responsibilities of teaching can be demanding indeed. When I feel tired or discouraged, let me turn my thoughts and my prayers to you. Let me always trust Your promises, Father, and let me draw strength from those promises and from Your unending love. Amen

SERVICE

Sitting down, He called the Twelve and said to them, "If anyone wants to be first, he must be last of all and servant of all."

Mark 9:35 Holman CSB

Jesus teaches that the most esteemed men and women are not the leaders of society or the captains of industry. To the contrary, Jesus teaches that the greatest among us are those who choose to minister and to serve.

Today, you may feel the temptation to build yourself up in the eyes of your neighbors. Resist that temptation. Instead, serve your neighbors quietly and without fanfare. Find a need and fill it . . . humbly. Lend a helping hand and share a word of kindness . . . anonymously.

Today, take the time to minister to those in need. Then, when you have done your best to serve your neighbors and to serve your God, you can rest comfortably knowing that in the eyes of God you have achieved greatness. And God's eyes, after all, are the only ones that really count.

Doing something positive toward another person is a practical approach to feeling good about yourself.

Barbara Johnson

YOUR TALENTS

Do not neglect the gift that is in you.

1 Timothy 4:14 Holman CSB

Make no mistake—God knew precisely what He was doing when He gave you a unique set of talents and opportunities. And now, God wants you to use those talents for the glory of His kingdom. So here's the big question: will you choose to use those talents, or not?

Being a godly teacher in today's difficult world requires insight, discipline, patience, and prayer. May you, with God's help, use your talents to touch the hearts and minds of your students and, in doing so, refashion this wonderful world . . . and the next.

God often reveals His direction for our lives through the way He made us . . . with a certain personality and unique skills.

Bill Hybels

—TODAY'S PRAYER—

Father, You have given me abilities to be used for the glory of Your kingdom. Give me the courage and the perseverance to use those talents. Keep me mindful that all my gifts come from You, Lord. Let me be Your faithful, humble servant, and let me give You all the glory and all the praise. Amen

HIS PROTECTION

We are pressured in every way but not crushed; we are perplexed but not in despair.

2 Corinthians 4:8 Holman CSB

From time to time, all of us have to face troubles and disappointments. When we do, God stands ready to protect us. Psalm 147 promises, "He heals the brokenhearted" (v. 3, NIV), but it doesn't say that He heals them instantly. Usually, it takes time for God to heal His children.

If you find yourself in any kind of trouble, pray about it and ask God for help. And then be patient. God will work things out, just as He has promised, but He will do it in His own time and according to His own plan.

God takes us through struggles and difficulties so that we might become increasingly committed to Him.

Charles Swindoll

—TODAY'S PRAYER—

Heavenly Father, You are my strength and my refuge. As I journey through this day, I know that I may encounter disappointments and losses. When I am troubled, let me turn to You. Keep me steady, Lord, and renew a right spirit inside of me this day and forever. Amen

YOUR ATTITUDE

Make your own attitude that of Christ Jesus.

Philippians 2:5 Holman CSB

What's your attitude today? Are you fearful, angry, bored, or worried? Are you worried more about pleasing your friends than about pleasing your God? Are you confused, bitter or pessimistic? If so, God wants to have a little talk with you.

God created you in His own image, and He wants you to experience joy and abundance. But, God will not force His joy upon you; you must claim it for yourself. So today, and every day thereafter, celebrate this life that God has given you. Think optimistically about yourself and your future. Give thanks to the One who has given you everything, and trust in your heart that He wants to give you so much more.

—TODAY'S PRAYER—

Lord, I pray for an attitude that is Christlike. Whatever my circumstances, whether good or bad, triumphal or tragic, let my response reflect a God-honoring attitude of optimism, faith, and love for You. Amen

CHANGE

John said, "Change your hearts and lives because the kingdom of heaven is near."

Matthew 3:2 NCV

Our world is in a state of constant change, and so, too, is the teaching profession. At times, the world seems to be trembling beneath our feet. But we can be comforted in the knowledge that our Heavenly Father is the rock that cannot be shaken. His Word promises, "I am the Lord, I do not change" (Malachi 3:6 NKJV).

Every day that we live, we mortals encounter a multitude of changes—some good, some not so good. And on occasion, all of us must endure life-changing personal losses that leave us breathless. When we do, our loving Heavenly Father stands ready to protect us, to comfort us, to guide us, and, in time, to heal us.

Are you facing difficult circumstances or unwelcome changes? If so, please remember that God is far bigger than any problem you may face. So, instead of worrying about life's inevitable challenges, put your faith in the Father and His only begotten Son: "Jesus Christ is the same yesterday, today, and forever" (Hebrews 13:8 Holman CSB). And rest assured: It is precisely because your Savior does not change that you can face your challenges with courage for this day and hope for the future.

HIS POWER

For the kingdom of God is not in talk but in power.

1 Corinthians 4:20 Holman CSB

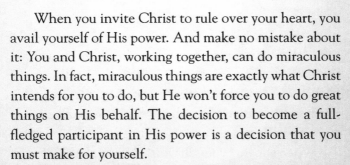

When you invite Christ to rule over your heart, you avail yourself of His power. And make no mistake about it: You and Christ, working together, can do miraculous things. In fact, miraculous things are exactly what Christ intends for you to do, but He won't force you to do great things on His behalf. The decision to become a full-fledged participant in His power is a decision that you must make for yourself.

The words of John 14:12 make this promise: when you put absolute faith in Christ, you can share in His power. Today, trust the Savior's promise and expect a miracle in His name.

God is able to make a way out of no way and transform dark yesterdays into bright tomorrows. This is our hope for becoming better men and women. This is our mandate for seeking to make a better world.

Martin Luther King, Jr.

—TODAY'S PRAYER—

Dear Lord, Your Son died for the salvation of all men and women, and He died for me. Through the power of Christ, I can be compassionate, courageous, and strong. Help me use that power, Father, for the glory of Your kingdom, today and forever. Amen

LIVE COURAGEOUSLY

Therefore, being always of good courage . . . we walk by faith, not by sight.

2 Corinthians 5:6-7 NASB

Christians have every reason to live courageously. After all, the ultimate battle has already been won on the cross at Calvary. But even dedicated followers of Christ may find their courage tested by the inevitable disappointments and fears that visit the lives of believers and non-believers alike.

When you find yourself worried about the challenges of today or the uncertainties of tomorrow, you must ask yourself whether or not you are ready to place your concerns and your life in God's all-powerful, all-knowing, all-loving hands. If the answer to that question is yes— as it should be—then you can draw courage today from the source of strength that never fails: your Heavenly Father.

Our Lord is searching for people who will make a difference. Christians dare not dissolve into the background or blend into the neutral scenery of the world.

Charles Swindoll

WE'RE ALL HUMAN

A person's insight gives him patience, and his virtue is to overlook an offense.

Proverbs 19:11 Holman CSB

All of us can be grumpy, hardheaded, and difficult to deal with at times. And as teachers, we must, from time to time, encounter out-of-sorts parents or their out-of-sorts offspring. When you have occasion to deal with difficult people (and you will), don't allow yourself to become caught up in the other person's emotional outbursts. If someone is ranting, raving, or worse, you have the right to excuse yourself and leave. Remember: emotions are highly contagious, so if the other person is angry, you will soon become angry, too. Instead of adding your own emotional energy to the outburst, you should make the conscious effort to remain calm—and part of remaining calm may be leaving the scene.

When you've finished dealing with that difficult person, do your best to forget about the confrontation. Everybody's human, and everybody needs forgiveness. And that includes, parents, students, and—on rare occasions—teachers, too.

When something robs you of your peace of mind, ask yourself if it is worth the energy you are expending on it. If not, then put it out of your mind in an act of discipline. Every time the thought of "it" returns, refuse it.

Kay Arthur

ENCOURAGEMENT

Therefore encourage one another and build each other up as you are already doing.

1 Thessalonians 5:11 Holman CSB

Hope, like other human emotions, is contagious. If you associate with hope-filled, enthusiastic people, their enthusiasm will have a tendency to lift your spirits. But if you find yourself spending too much time in the company of naysayers, pessimists, or cynics, your thoughts, like theirs, will tend to be negative.

Are you a hopeful, optimistic Christian? And do you associate with like-minded people? If so, then you're availing yourself of a priceless gift: the encouragement of fellow believers. But, if you find yourself focusing on the negative aspects of life, perhaps it is time to search out a few new friends.

As a faithful follower of the man from Galilee, you have every reason to be hopeful. So today, look for reasons to celebrate God's endless blessings. And while you're at it, look for people who will join with you in the celebration. You'll be better for their company, and they'll be better for yours.

Words. Do you fully understand their power? Can any of us really grasp the mighty force behind the things we say? Do we stop and think before we speak, considering the potency of the words we utter?

Joni Eareckson Tada

TEACHING BY EXAMPLE

We have around us many people whose lives tell us what faith means. So let us run the race that is before us and never give up. We should remove from our lives anything that would get in the way and the sin that so easily holds us back.

Hebrews 12:1 NCV

We teach our students by the words we speak and the lives we lead, but not necessarily in that order. Sometimes, our actions speak so loudly that they drown out our words completely. That's why, as teachers, we must make certain that the lives we lead are in harmony with the lessons we preach.

Are you the kind of teacher whose life serves as a powerful example of righteousness and godliness? If so, you are also a powerful force for good in your classroom and in your world.

Phillips Brooks advised, "Be such a man, and live such a life, that if every man were such as you, and every life a life like yours, this earth would be God's Paradise." And that's sound advice because our families and our students are watching . . . and so, for that matter, is God.

It is a great deal better to live a holy life than to talk about it. Lighthouses do not ring bells and fire cannons to call attention to their shining—they just shine.

D. L. Moody

FORGIVING FAMILY MEMBERS

A constantly squabbling family disintegrates.

Mark 3:24 MSG

How often must we forgive family members and friends? More times than we can count. Our children are precious but imperfect; so are our spouses and our friends. We must, on occasion, forgive those who have injured us; to do otherwise is to disobey God. If there exists even one person, alive or dead, whom you have not forgiven (and that includes yourself), follow God's commandment and His will for your life: forgive. Hatred and bitterness and regret are not part of God's plan for your life. Forgiveness is.

There is always room for more loving forgiveness within our homes.

James Dobson

Forgiveness is God's command.

Martin Luther

—TODAY'S PRAYER—

Dear Lord, You have blessed me with a family to love and to care for. Protect my family, Lord. And, let me show them love, forgiveness, and acceptance, so that through me they might come to know You. Amen

EYES ON HIM

Keep your eyes on Jesus, who both began and finished this race we're in. Study how he did it. Because he never lost sight of where he was headed—that exhilarating finish in and with God—he could put up with anything along the way: cross, shame, whatever. And now he's there, in the place of honor, right alongside God.

Hebrews 12:2 MSG

Jesus has called upon believers of every generation (and that includes you) to follow in His footsteps. And God's Word promises that when you follow in Christ's footsteps, you will learn how to live freely and lightly (Matthew 11:28-30).

With whom will you choose to walk today? Will you walk with shortsighted people who honor the ways of the world, or will you walk with the Son of God? Jesus walks with you. Are you walking with Him? Hopefully, you will choose to walk with Him today and every day of your life.

Jesus doesn't want you to be a run-of-the-mill, follow-the-crowd kind of believer. Jesus wants you to be a "new creation" through Him. And that's exactly what you should want for yourself, too. Jesus deserves your extreme enthusiasm; the world deserves it; and you deserve the experience of sharing it.

YOUR BRIGHT FUTURE

I say this because I know what I am planning for you," says the Lord. "I have good plans for you, not plans to hurt you. I will give you hope and a good future."

Jeremiah 29:11 NCV

How bright is your future? Well, if you're a faithful believer, God's plans for you are so bright that you'd better wear shades. But here's an important question: How bright do you believe your future to be? Are you expecting a terrific tomorrow, or are you dreading a terrible one? The answer you give will have a powerful impact on the way tomorrow turns out.

Do you trust in the ultimate goodness of God's plan for your life? Will you face tomorrow's challenges with optimism and hope? You should. After all, God created you for a very important reason: His reason. And you still have important work to do: His work.

Today, as you live in the present and look to the future, remember that God has an amazing plan for you. Act—and believe—accordingly.

—TODAY'S PRAYER—

Dear Lord, as I look to the future, I will place my trust in You. If I become discouraged, I will turn to You. If I am afraid, I will seek strength in You. You are my Father, and I will place my hope, my trust, and my faith in You. Amen

GOD'S MERCY

For the LORD your God is a merciful God....
                                                                Deuteronomy 4:31 NIV

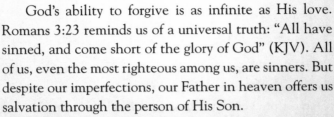

God's ability to forgive is as infinite as His love. Romans 3:23 reminds us of a universal truth: "All have sinned, and come short of the glory of God" (KJV). All of us, even the most righteous among us, are sinners. But despite our imperfections, our Father in heaven offers us salvation through the person of His Son.

God sent Jesus to die so that we might have eternal life. As Christians, we have been blessed by a merciful, loving God. May we accept His mercy. And may we, in turn, show love and mercy to our friends, to our families, and to all whom He chooses to place in our paths.

God loves you, and He yearns for you to turn away from the path of evil. You need His forgiveness, and you need Him to come into your life and remake you from within.

Billy Graham

There are some facts that will never change. One fact is that you are forgiven. He sees you better than you see yourself. And that is a glorious fact of your life.

Max Lucado

YOUR LAMP?

All Scripture is inspired by God and is profitable for teaching, for rebuking, for correcting, for training in righteousness, so that the man of God may be complete, equipped for every good work.

2 Timothy 3:16-17 Holman CSB

Is God's Word a lamp that guides your behavior in the classroom and beyond? Is God's Word your indispensable compass for everyday living, or is it relegated to Sunday morning services? Do you read the Bible faithfully or sporadically? The answer to these questions will determine the direction of your thoughts, the direction of your day, and the direction of your life.

God's Word is unlike any other book. The Bible is a roadmap for life here on earth and for life eternal. As Christians, we are called upon to study God's Holy Word, to trust its promises, to follow its commandments, and to share its Good News with the world.

As believers, we must study the Bible and meditate upon its meaning for our lives. Otherwise, we deprive ourselves of a priceless gift from our Creator. God's Holy Word is, indeed, a transforming, life-changing, one-of-a-kind treasure. And, a passing acquaintance with the Good Book is insufficient for Christians who seek to obey God's Word and to understand His will. After all, neither man nor woman should live by bread alone . . .

HABITS

Do not be deceived: "Evil company corrupts good habits."
1 Corinthians 15:33 NKJV

It's an old saying and a true one: First, you make your habits, and then your habits make you. Some habits will inevitably bring you closer to God; other habits will lead you away from the path He has chosen for you. If you sincerely desire to improve your spiritual health, you must honestly examine the habits that make up the fabric of your day. And you must abandon those habits that are displeasing to God.

If you trust God, and if you keep asking for His help, He can transform your life. If you sincerely ask Him to help you, the same God who created the universe will help you defeat the harmful habits that have heretofore defeated you. So, if at first you don't succeed, keep praying. God is listening, and He's ready to help you become a better person if you ask Him . . . so ask today.

You will never change your life until you change something you do daily.

John Maxwell

—TODAY'S PRAYER—

Dear Lord, help me break bad habits and form good ones. And let my actions be pleasing to You, today and every day. Amen

LIKE A RIVER

I've loved you the way my Father has loved me. Make yourselves at home in my love.

John 15:9 MSG

Jesus offers you a love that is boundless and eternal. Your task is to receive His love . . . starting now.

Christ is like a river that is continually flowing. There are always fresh supplies of water coming from the fountain-head, so that a man may live by it and be supplied with water all his life. So Christ is an ever-flowing fountain; he is continually supplying his people, and the fountain is not spent. They who live upon Christ may have fresh supplies from him for all eternity; they may have an increase of blessedness that is new, and new still, and which never will come to an end.

Jonathan Edwards

—TODAY'S PRAYER—

Heavenly Father, Your Word instructs me to walk in integrity and in truth. Make me a worthy teacher, Lord. Let my words be true, and let my actions lead my students to You. Amen

GOOD ADVICE

The lips of the righteous feed many.

Proverbs 10:21 Holman CSB

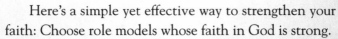

Here's a simple yet effective way to strengthen your faith: Choose role models whose faith in God is strong.

When you emulate godly people, you become a more godly person yourself. That's why you should seek out mentors who, by their words and their presence, make you a better person and a better Christian.

Today, as a gift to yourself, select, from your friends and family members, a mentor whose judgment you trust. Then listen carefully to your mentor's advice and be willing to accept that advice, even if accepting it requires effort, or pain, or both. Consider your mentor to be God's gift to you. Thank God for that gift, and use it for the glory of His kingdom.

—TODAY'S PRAYER—

Dear Lord, thank You for the mentors whom You have placed along my path. When I am troubled, let me turn to them for help, for guidance, for comfort, and for perspective. And Father, let me be a friend and mentor to others, so that my love for You may be demonstrated by my genuine concern for them. Amen

PASSION

He did it with all his heart. So he prospered.

2 Chronicles 31:21 NKJV

Are you excited about your career? Do you consider the teaching profession to be a worthy life's work? Does your job make you want to hop out of bed in the morning and get to work? And are you convinced that you're making the world a better place for your students and yourself? If so, thank God every day for that blessing.

But what if you have not yet discovered the "perfect" job? If so, don't allow yourself to become discouraged. Instead, keep searching and keep trusting that with God's help, you can—and will—find a meaningful way to serve your neighbors, your students, and your God.

—TODAY'S PRAYER—

Lord, let me find my strength in You. When I am weary, give me rest. When I feel overwhelmed, let me look to You for my priorities. Let Your passion be my passion, Lord, and let Your way be my way, today and forever. Amen

PLANNING

The plans of hard-working people earn a profit, but those who act too quickly become poor.

Proverbs 21:5 NCV

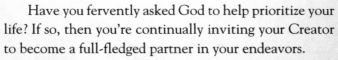

Have you fervently asked God to help prioritize your life? If so, then you're continually inviting your Creator to become a full-fledged partner in your endeavors.

When you make God's priorities your priorities, you will receive God's abundance and His peace. When you make God a full partner in every aspect of your life, He will lead you along the proper path: His path. When you allow God to play a role in the organization of your day, He will honor you with spiritual blessings that are simply too numerous to count. So, as you plan for the day ahead, take a few quiet moments to gather your thoughts and consult your Creator. It's the best way to plan your day and your life.

—TODAY'S PRAYER—

Dear Lord, help me accept the past, help me enjoy the present, and help me plan for the future. While I am doing these things, help me to trust You more and more . . . this day and every day. Amen

PURPOSE

We look at this Son and see the God who cannot be seen. We look at this Son and see God's original purpose in everything created.

Colossians 1:15 MSG

God has things He wants you to do and places He wants you to go. The most important decision of your life is, of course, your commitment to accept Jesus Christ as your personal Lord and Savior. And, once your eternal destiny is secured, you will undoubtedly ask yourself the question "What now, Lord?" If you earnestly seek God's will for your life, you will find it . . . in time.

As you seek to discover God's path for your life, you should study His Holy Word and be ever watchful for His signs. You should associate with fellow Christians who will encourage your spiritual growth, and you should listen to that inner voice that speaks to you in the quiet moments of your daily devotionals.

Rest assured: God is here, and He intends to use you in wonderful, unexpected ways. He desires to lead you along a path of His choosing. Your challenge is to watch, to listen . . . and to follow.

Whatever purpose motivates your life, it must be something big enough and grand enough to make the investment worthwhile.

Warren Wiersbe

SAD DAYS

Those people who know they have great spiritual needs are happy, because the kingdom of heaven belongs to them. Those who are sad now are happy, because God will comfort them.

Matthew 5:3-4 NCV

Some days are light and happy, and some days are not. When we face the inevitable dark days of life, we must choose how we will respond. Will we allow ourselves to sink even more deeply into our own sadness, or will we do the difficult work of pulling ourselves out? We bring light to the dark days of life by turning first to God, and then to trusted family members and friends. Then, we must go to work solving the problems that confront us. When we do, the clouds will eventually part, and the sun will shine once more upon our souls.

When we cry, we allow our bodies to function according to God's design—and we embrace one of the "perks" he offers to relieve our stress.

Barbara Johnson

Emotions we have not poured out in the safe hands of God can turn into feelings of hopelessness and depression. God is safe.

Beth Moore

WHOLESOME TALK

To everything there is a season . . . a time to keep silence, and a time to speak.

Ecclesiastes 3:1,7 KJV

This world can be a difficult place, a place where many of our friends and family members are troubled by the inevitable challenges of everyday life. And since we can never be certain who needs our help, we should be careful to speak helpful words to everybody who crosses our paths.

In the book of Ephesians, Paul writes, "Do not let any unwholesome talk come out of your mouths, but only what is helpful for building others up according to their needs, that it may benefit those who listen" (4:29 NIV). Paul reminds us that when we choose our words carefully, we can have a powerful impact on those around us.

Today, let's share kind words, smiles, encouragement, and hugs with family, with friends, and with the world.

When you talk, choose the very same words that you would use if Jesus were looking over your shoulder. Because He is.

Marie T. Freeman

GRIEF

I have heard your prayer; I have seen your tears. Look, I will heal you.

2 Kings 20:5 Holman CSB

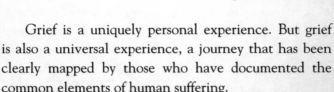

Grief is a uniquely personal experience. But grief is also a universal experience, a journey that has been clearly mapped by those who have documented the common elements of human suffering.

Grief usually begins with shock and then gives way to intense pain. Over time, as the mourner regains his or her emotional balance, the pain begins to fade. Gradually, a new life is raised from the ashes of the old. Christians face grief armed with God's promises. Through the Holy Bible, He promises to comfort and heal those who call upon Him.

As you experience the searing pain of any significant loss, knowledge is power. The more you understand the grieving process, the better you can cope with its many twists and turns. But whatever the nature of your loss, always remember this overriding truth: God is with you, God is good, and you are protected.

Suffering may be someone's fault or it may not be anyone's fault. But if given to God, our suffering becomes an opportunity to experience the power of God at work in our lives and to give glory to Him.

Anne Graham Lotz

TRUSTING GOD

He granted their request because they trusted in Him.

1 Chronicles 5:20 Holman CSB

Sometimes the future seems bright, and sometimes it does not. Yet even when we cannot see the possibilities of tomorrow, God can. As believers, our challenge is to trust an uncertain future to an all-powerful God.

When we trust God, we should trust Him without reservation. We should steel ourselves against the inevitable disappointments of the day, secure in the knowledge that our Heavenly Father has a plan for the future that only He can see.

Can you place your future into the hands of a loving and all-knowing God? Can you live amid the uncertainties of today, knowing that God has dominion over all your tomorrows? If you can, you are wise and you are blessed. When you trust God with everything you are and everything you have, He will bless you now and forever.

Ten thousand enemies cannot stop a Christian, cannot even slow him down, if he meets them in an attitude of complete trust in God.

A. W. Tozer

WORRY

Give all your worries and cares to God, for he cares about what happens to you.

1 Peter 5:6 NLT

Because we are imperfect human beings, we worry. Even though we are Christians who have been given the assurance of salvation—even though we are Christians who have received the promise of God's love and protection—we find ourselves fretting over the countless details of everyday life. Jesus understood our concerns when He spoke the reassuring words found in Matthew 6: "Therefore I tell you, do not worry about your life . . ."

As you consider the promises of Jesus, remember that God still sits in His heaven and you are His beloved child. Then, perhaps, you will worry a little less and trust God a little more, and that's as it should be because God is trustworthy . . . and you are protected.

—TODAY'S PRAYER—

Dear Lord, wherever I find myself, let me celebrate more and worry less. When my faith begins to waver, help me to trust You more. Then, with praise on my lips and the love of Your Son in my heart, let me live courageously, faithfully, prayerfully, and thankfully this day and every day. Amen

LAUGHTER

There is an occasion for everything, and a time for every activity under heaven . . . a time to weep and a time to laugh; a time to mourn and a time to dance.

Ecclesiastes 3:1,4 Holman CSB

Laughter is a gift from God, a gift that He intends for us to use. Yet sometimes, because of the inevitable stresses of everyday living, we fail to find the fun in life. When we allow life's inevitable disappointments to cast a pall over our lives and our souls, we do a profound disservice to ourselves and to our loved ones.

If you've allowed the clouds of life to obscure the blessings of life, perhaps you've formed the unfortunate habit of taking things just a little too seriously. If so, it's time to fret a little less and laugh a little more.

So today, look for the humor that most certainly surrounds you—when you do, you'll find it. And remember: God created laughter for a reason . . . and Father indeed knows best. So laugh!

A keen sense of humor helps us to overlook the unbecoming, understand the unconventional, tolerate the unpleasant, overcome the unexpected, and outlast the unbearable.

Billy Graham

GOD'S SUPPORT

I am holding you by your right hand—I, the LORD your God. And I say to you, "Do not be afraid. I am here to help you...."

Isaiah 41:13 NLT

God is a never-ending source of support and courage for those of us who call upon Him. When we are weary, He gives us strength. When we see no hope, God reminds us of His promises. When we grieve, God wipes away our tears.

Do the demands of this day threaten to overwhelm you? If so, you must rely not only upon your own resources but also upon the promises of your Father in heaven. God will hold your hand and walk with you every day of your life if you let Him. So even if your circumstances are difficult, trust the Father. His love is eternal and His goodness endures forever.

—TODAY'S PRAYER—

Lord, You have promised never to leave me or forsake me. You are always with me, protecting me and encouraging me. Whatever this day may bring, I thank You for Your love and for Your strength. Let me lean upon You, Father, this day and forever. Amen

HE IS GOD

He is the Lord. He will do what He thinks is good.

1 Samuel 3:18 Holman CSB

Sometimes, we must accept life on its terms, not our own. Life has a way of unfolding, not as we will, but as it will. And sometimes, there is precious little we can do to change things.

When events transpire that are beyond our control, we have a choice: we can either learn the art of acceptance, or we can make ourselves miserable as we struggle to change the unchangeable.

We must entrust the things we cannot change to God. Once we have done so, we can prayerfully and faithfully tackle the important work that He has placed before us: the things we can change.

—TODAY'S PRAYER—

Father, the events of this world unfold according to a plan that I cannot fully understand. But You understand. Help me to trust You, Lord, even when I am grieving. Help me to trust You even when I am confused. Today, in whatever circumstances I find myself, let me trust Your will and accept Your love . . . completely. Amen

ARGUMENTS

And a servant of the Lord must not quarrel but be gentle to all, able to teach, patient.

2 Timothy 2:24 NKJV

Arguments are seldom won but often lost. When we engage in petty squabbles, our losses usually outpace our gains. When we acquire the unfortunate habit of habitual bickering, we do harm to our friends, to our families, to our coworkers, and to ourselves.

Time and again, God's Word warns us that most arguments are a monumental waste of time, of energy, of life. In Titus, we are warned to refrain from "foolish arguments," and with good reason. Such arguments usually do more for the devil than they do for God.

So the next time you're tempted to engage in a silly squabble, whether inside the church or outside it, refrain. When you do, you'll put a smile on God's face, and you'll send the devil packing.

Divisions between Christians are a sin and a scandal, and Christians ought at all times to be making contributions toward reunion, if it is only by their prayers.

C. S. Lewis

BORN AGAIN

Jesus answered and said to him, "Truly, truly, I say to you, unless one is born again he cannot see the kingdom of God."

John 3:3 NASB

Why did Christ die on the cross? Christ sacrificed His life so that we might be born again. This gift, freely given from God's only begotten Son, is the priceless possession of everyone who accepts Him as Lord and Savior.

God is waiting patiently for each of us to accept the gift of eternal life. Let us claim Christ's gift today. Let us walk with the Savior, let us love Him, let us praise Him, and let us share His message of salvation with all those who cross our paths.

The comforting words of Ephesians 2:8 make God's promise clear: "For by grace you have been saved through faith, and that not of yourselves; it is the gift of God" (NKJV). Thus, we are saved not because of our good deeds but because of our faith in Christ. May we, who have been given so much, praise our Savior for the gift of salvation, and may we share the joyous news of our Master's limitless love with our families, with our friends, and with the world.

Being born again is God's solution to our need for love and life and light.

Anne Graham Lotz

PRECIOUS RESOURCES

The disciples shooed them off. But Jesus was irate and let them know it: "Don't push these children away. Don't ever get between them and me. These children are at the very center of life in the kingdom. Mark this: Unless you accept God's kingdom in the simplicity of a child, you'll never get in."

Mark 10:14-15 MSG

Our children are this nation's most precious resource. And, as responsible adults, we must create a homeland in which the next generation of Americans can live in safety and in freedom. Thankfully, the American Dream is alive and well; it is our responsibility to ensure that it remains so. We must protect our nation's liberties with the same sense of dedication and urgency that our forebears demonstrated when they earned those liberties on the fields of battle and in the halls of justice.

Today, let us pray for our children . . . all of them. Let us pray for children here at home and for children around the world. Every child is God's child. May we, as concerned adults, behave—and pray—accordingly.

Children must be valued as our most priceless possession.

James Dobson

YOU CHANGE THE WORLD

Instruct and direct one another using good common sense. And sing, sing your hearts out to God! Let every detail in your lives—words, actions, whatever—be done in the name of the Master, Jesus, thanking God the Father every step of the way.

Colossians 3:16-17 MSG

Oh, the glorious opportunities that are available to those who teach. May you, with God's help, touch the hearts and minds of your students and, in doing so, refashion this wonderful world…and the next.

If we work in marble, it will perish; if we work upon brass, time will efface it; if we rear temples, they will crumble into dust; but if we work upon immortal minds and instill in them just principles, we are then engraving upon tablets which no time will efface, but will brighten and brighten to all eternity.

Daniel Webster

—TODAY'S PRAYER—

Heavenly Father, Your Word tells us that teachers are judged strictly and that I have an awesome responsibility to lead my students in the way of truth. Lord, I ask for Your help today as I prepare to teach. May I speak the truth, may I be a worthy example to those who watch my behavior, and may the glory be Yours. Amen

SHARING

If you have two coats, give one to the poor. If you have food, share it with those who are hungry.

Luke 3:11 NLT

Sometimes, amid the busyness and distractions of this complicated world, we may fail to share our possessions, our talents, or our time. Yet, God commands that we treat others as we wish to be treated. God's Word makes it clear: we must be generous with others just as we seek generosity for ourselves.

As believers in Christ, we are blessed here on earth, and we are blessed eternally through God's grace. We can never fully repay God for His gifts, but we can share them with others. When we give sacrificially, our blessings are multiplied . . . and so is our joy.

The measure of a life, after all, is not its duration but its donation.

Corrie ten Boom

—TODAY'S PRAYER—

Lord, I know there is no happiness in keeping Your blessings for myself. True joy is found in sharing what I have with others. Make me a generous and obedient servant, and let me share my blessings with my family, with my friends, and with all those whom You have seen fit to place along my path. Amen

THANK YOU

Be conscientious about yourself and your teaching; persevere in these things, for by doing this you will save both yourself and your hearers.

1 Timothy 4:13 Holman CSB

As a concerned teacher, you have earned the undying gratitude of countless students and their families. Because you have chosen to teach, you have touched many lives and shaped many minds. For all your hard work and sacrifices, you've earned a heartfelt "Thank you!"

May you, with God's help, continue to share His blessings with your students and with the world.

Teaching is a divine calling. Whether we teach at home, at church, or in a school classroom, transfer of knowledge is a significant undertaking.

Suzanne Dale Ezell

—TODAY'S PRAYER—

Dear Lord, there is so much to teach and so little time. Let me share Your wisdom with my students, with my family, and with the world. And, let my love for You be evident in the lessons that I teach and the life that I live. Amen

NOTES

NOTES